REJOICE: CELEBRATING THE SEASON OF ADVENT

Copyright © 2024 by Love God Greatly Ministry

Permission is granted to print and reproduce this document for the purpose of completing the *Rejoice: Celebrating the season of Advent* online Bible study. Please do not alter this document in any way. All rights reserved. Published in Dallas by Love God Greatly.

Photo source:
unsplash.com

Recipe source:
Renita, LGG Albanian Branch

Information and data source:
Joshua Project, joshuaproject.net/languages/als, accessed April 2024.

Unless otherwise directed in writing by the Publisher, Scripture quotations are from the NET BIBLE® translation, copyright 2019, by Bible.org. Used by permission. All rights reserved.

Published in the United States of America, Library of Congress Catalogue-in-Publication data,

ISBN 979-8-3338563-5-7

29	28	27	26	25	24
6	5	4	3	2	1

WHEN WOMEN ARE
EQUIPPED WITH THE
KNOWLEDGE OF GOD'S
TRUTH, THE WORLD
IS TRANSFORMED ONE
WOMAN AT A TIME.

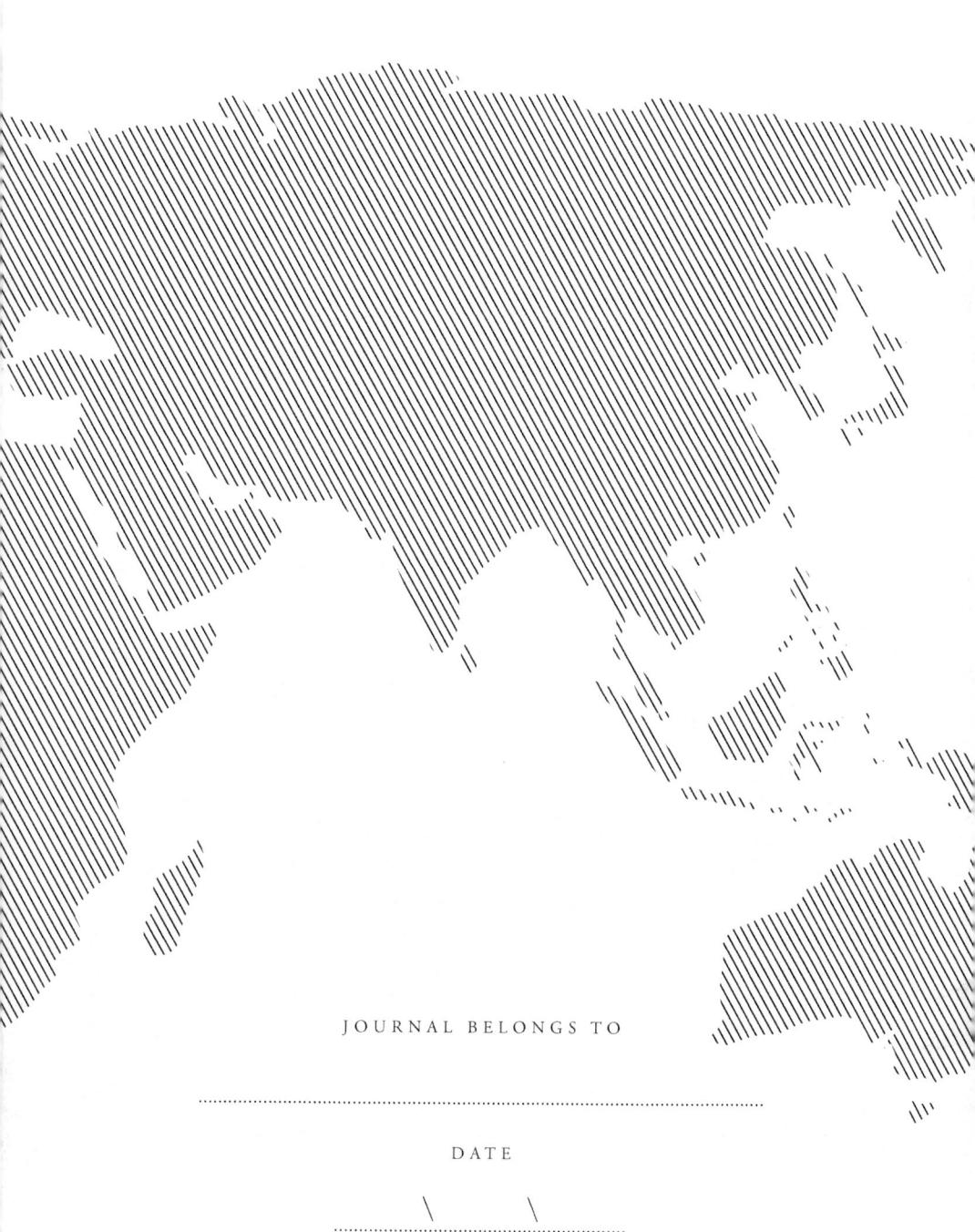

CONTENTS

003 WELCOME
005 ABOUT LGG
006 OUR MISSION
008 SOAP BIBLE STUDY METHOD
013 TESTIMONY
014 GLOBAL OUTREACH
016 RECIPE
018 KNOW THESE TRUTHS
023 INTRODUCTION
024 READING PLAN
027 GOALS
029 WEEK 1
059 WEEK 2
085 WEEK 3
117 WEEK 4
145 JOIN US
147 FOR YOU

You
HAVE BEEN
PRAYED FOR;
IT IS NOT A
COINCIDENCE
YOU ARE
PARTICIPATING
IN THIS
STUDY.

WELCOME, FRIEND!

We are glad you have decided to join us in this Bible study! You have been prayed for; it is not a coincidence you are participating in this study.

Our prayer for you is simple: that you will grow closer to our Lord as you dig into His Word each and every day. Each day before you read the assigned passage, pray and ask God to help you understand it. Invite Him to speak to you through His Word. Then listen. Believe He will be faithful to speak to you, and be faithful to listen and obey.

Take time to read the verses over and over again. The Bible tells us that if we seek wisdom like silver and search for it like hidden treasure, then we will understand how to fear the Lord, and we will discover knowledge about God (Proverbs 2:4–5).

All of us here at Love God Greatly can't wait for you to get started, and we hope to see you at the finish line. Endure, persevere, press on; don't give up! Finish well what you are beginning today.

We will be here cheering for you every step of the way! We are in this together. Be expectant that God has much in store for you in this study. Journey with us as we learn to love God greatly with our lives!

WE NEED EACH OTHER, AND WE LIVE LIFE BETTER TOGETHER. WOULD YOU CONSIDER REACHING OUT AND DOING THIS STUDY WITH SOMEONE?

ABOUT LGG

Love God Greatly exists to inspire, encourage, and equip women around the world to love God greatly with their lives.

INSPIRE women to make God's Word a priority in their daily lives through Bible study resources.

ENCOURAGE women in their walks with God through online community and personal accountability.

EQUIP women to grow in their faith so they can effectively reach others for Christ.

We start with a simple Bible reading plan, but it doesn't stop there. Some women gather in homes and churches locally, while others connect online with women across the globe. Whatever the method, we lovingly lock arms and unite for this purpose: to love God greatly with our lives.

At Love God Greatly, you'll find real, authentic women. You'll find women who desire less of each other, and a whole lot more of Jesus. Women who long to know God through His Word because we believe that truth transforms and sets us free. Women who are better together, saturated in God's Word and in community with one another.

Love God Greatly is committed to providing quality Bible study materials and believes finances should never get in the way of a woman being able to participate in one of our studies.

Our journals and other resources are available for purchase in our website store. A few of our journals are also available through Amazon. Search for "Love God Greatly" to see all of our Bible study journals and books.

YOU'LL FIND WOMEN WHO ARE IMPERFECT, YET FORGIVEN.

Love God Greatly is a 501 (C) (3) non-profit organization. Funding for Love God Greatly comes through donations and proceeds from our online Bible study journals and books.

One-hundred percent of proceeds go directly back into supporting Love God Greatly and helping us inspire, encourage, and equip women all over the world with God's Word.

Arm-in-arm and hand-in-hand, let's do this together.

OUR MISSION

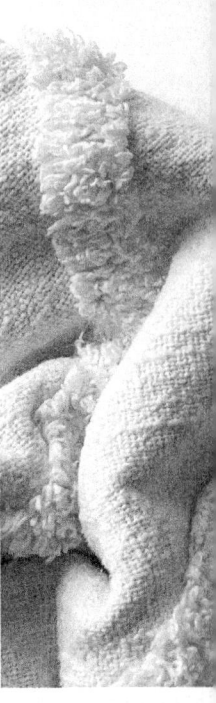

THE NEED

Billions of women around the world don't have access to God's Word in their native language. Those who do, don't have access to women's Bible studies designed and written with them in mind.

THE MISSION

At Love God Greatly, we create Bible studies in 45+ languages. We equip missionaries, ministries, local churches, and women with God's Word at an unprecedented rate by allowing our journals to be downloaded from our international sites at no cost.

Through studying the Bible in their own language with like-minded communities, women are trained and equipped with God's Word.

We believe when women read and apply God's Word to their lives and embrace His unchanging love for them, the world is a better place. We know one woman in God's Word can change a family, a community, and a nation... one woman at a time.

PARTNER WITH US

We would love for you to join us in our mission of giving women all over the world access to God's Word and quality Bible study resources! For any questions or for more information, email us or visit us online. We would love to hear from you!

INFO@LOVEGODGREATLY.COM

LOVEGODGREATLY.COM

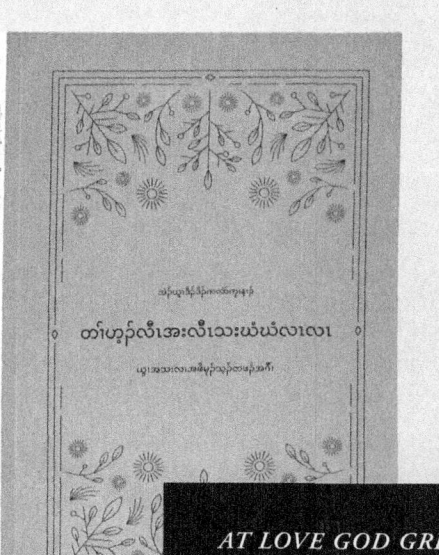

> AT LOVE GOD GREATLY,
> WE CREATE BIBLE STUDIES
> IN 45+ LANGUAGES.

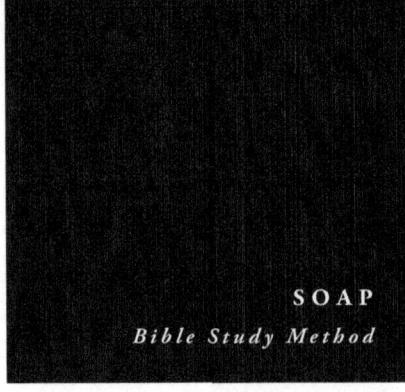

SOAP
Bible Study Method

At Love God Greatly, we believe that the Word of God is living and active. The words of Scripture are powerful and effective and relevant for life in all times and all cultures. In order to interpret the Bible correctly, we need an understanding of the context and culture of the original writings.

As we study the Bible, we use the SOAP Bible Study Method. The acronym stands for Scripture, Observation, Application, and Prayer. It's one thing to simply read Scripture. When you interact with it, intentionally slowing down to reflect, truths start jumping off the page. The SOAP Method allows us to dig deeper into Scripture and see more than we would if we simply read the verses. It allows us not only to be hearers of the Word, but doers as well (James 1:22).

YOU WILL NEVER WASTE TIME IN GOD'S WORD. IT IS LIVING, POWERFUL, AND EFFECTIVE, AND HE SPEAKS TO US THROUGH IT.

In this journal, we read a passage of Scripture and then apply the SOAP Method to specific verses. Using this method allows us to glean a greater understanding of Scripture, which allows us to apply it effectively to our lives.

The most important ingredients in the SOAP Method are your interaction with God's Word and your application of it to your life. Take time to study it carefully, discovering the truth of God's character and His heart for the world.

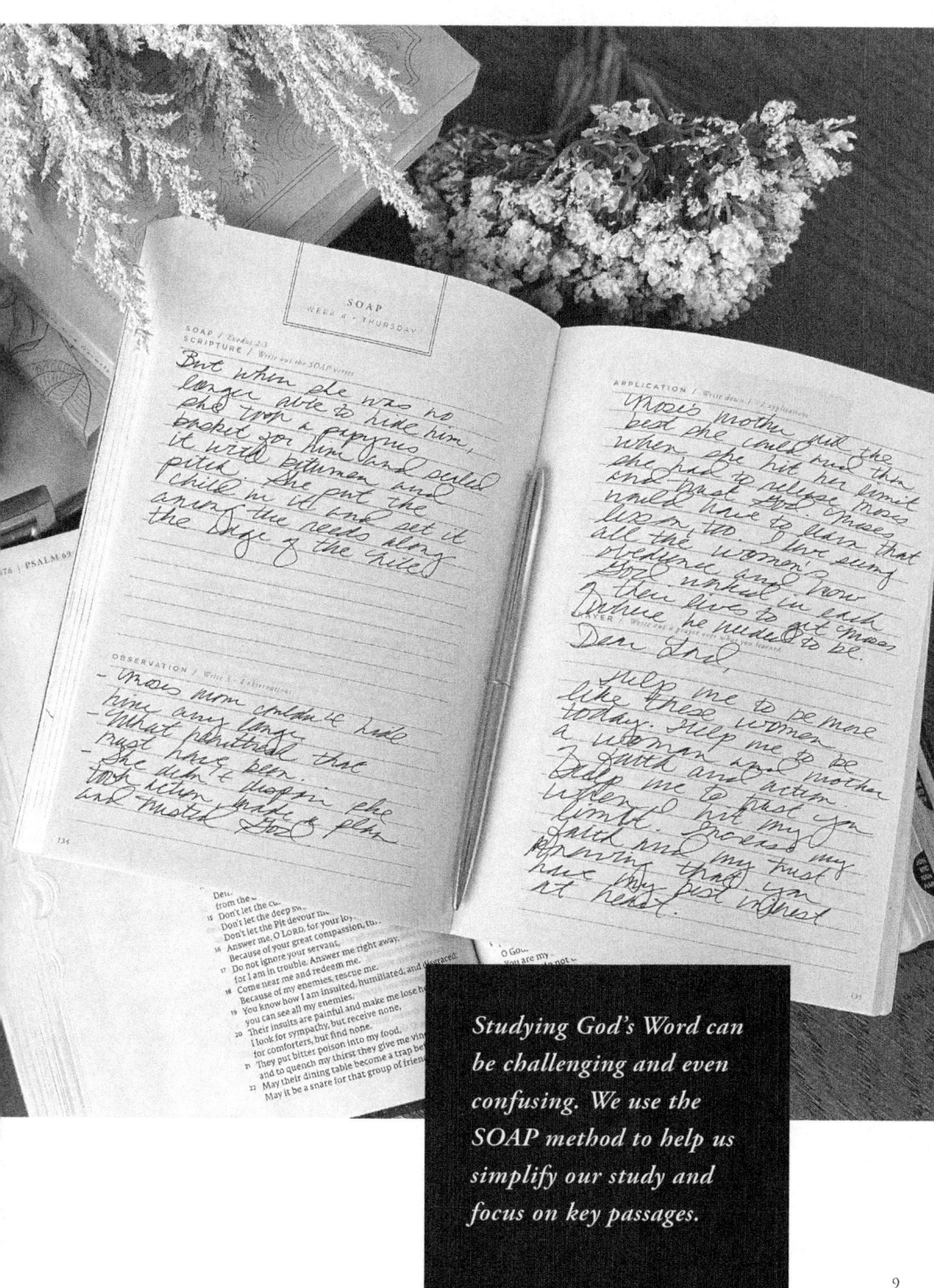

Studying God's Word can be challenging and even confusing. We use the SOAP method to help us simplify our study and focus on key passages.

SOAP
Bible Study Method

S

STANDS FOR SCRIPTURE

Physically write out the SOAP verses.

You'll be amazed at what God will reveal to you just by taking the time to slow down and write out what you are reading!

O

STANDS FOR OBSERVATION

What do you see in the verses that you're reading?

Who is the intended audience? Is there a repetition of words?

What words stand out to you?

A
STANDS FOR APPLICATION

This is when God's Word becomes personal.

What is God saying to you today? How can you apply what you just read to your own personal life?

What changes do you need to make? Is there action you need to take?

APPLICATION / *Write down 1 - 2 applications*

Remind myself of God's strength is more powerful than anything
Memorize these verses and say them daily this week
Ask God to strengthen my faith in Him
Trust God that he will deliver me from evil
Pray for my brothers and sister's in Christ

PRAYER / *Write out a prayer over what you learned*

Dear Lord,

Thank you for being constant, faithful, and loving towards me and my life. Help me to further my trust and faith in you daily and through difficult times.

Help me to know you're alway there by my side, guarding, and protecting me. Remind me of the suffering of others and to be able to help and encourage them in their growth.

I ask all these things in Jesus name.
Amen

P
STANDS FOR PRAYER

Pray God's Word back to Him.
Spend time thanking Him.

If He has revealed something to you during this time in His Word, pray about it.

If He has revealed some sin that is in your life, confess it. And remember, He loves you dearly.

LANGUAGE
HIGHLIGHT

TESTIMONY

LGG Albanian Branch

I was born in a country that was completely closed and isolated from the rest of the world because of the communist regime. Religion and religious practices were forbidden, and I had never heard of Christ or the Bible.

At the age of 9, the regime fell, so the first missionaries began to come to our country. My mom was eager to hear more about God, and she started attending the first meetings that were held in a house. She would always take me to the meetings where I would attend Sunday school. I found the Bible stories very interesting. I continued this routine for several years. Then one day, God spoke to me and touched my heart. I realized that these were not just stories. Jesus Christ really came to earth to save me and shed his blood for me. I realized I was living in a way that went against Christ, and I didn't want to do it anymore. I decided to give Him my heart and my life, dedicating myself and serving Him.

Today, it has been almost 30 years since that moment. God has blessed my life in a wonderful way. My heart's desire is to serve Him so that more would come to know Him.

A friend of mine had come into contact with the LGG studies. Using the SOAP method was a new way for us to study and know God more. We loved it so much that we first started using the studies by translating only the reading plans. I visited LGG's website and saw that the ministry didn't have any Albanian translations. God put a desire in my heart to translate these studies so that more Albanian women could use them.

GOD SPOKE TO ME AND TOUCHED MY HEART.

As we faithfully seek to translate each study, I pray that more and more Albanian women will come to know our Savior and be transformed.

Renita

LGG Albanian Branch

LANGUAGE	GLOBAL SPEAKERS	TO CONNECT WITH THIS BRANCH
Albanian	84,000	Email: ask@lovegodgreatly.com

UNITED STATES

LGG HOME

HOW CAN YOU PRAY FOR THIS BRANCH?

- For the LGG Albanian team to grow
- To be able to reach more women with Bible studies

WANT TO HELP?

ask@lovegodgreatly.com

LANGUAGE HIGHLIGHT

RECIPE

LGG Albanian Branch

Tave Kosi

ALBANIAN LAMB & YOGURT CASSEROLE

INGREDIENTS

2.2 LBS (1 KG) FRESH LAMB

4 ½ CUPS (1 KG) PLAIN YOGURT

2 TBSP FLOUR

3 EGGS

A LITTLE BUTTER

2 TBSP RICE

WATER

SALT

DIRECTIONS

Preheat oven to 425 F (220 C).

Put the meat in a pot. Add salt, a little butter, 2 tbsp rice, and enough water to cover the meat. Cook on medium heat until the meat is cooked.

Meanwhile, mix three eggs in a bowl. Add a little salt and 2 tbsp of flour. Mix well so that the flour does not become grainy. Add yogurt.

Once the lamb and rice mixture is cooled, mix in yogurt mixture.

Transfer ingredients to a baking pan or leave in an oven-safe pot. Cook in the oven until you get a golden color, in about 45-50 minutes.

KNOW THESE TRUTHS

GOD LOVES YOU

God's Word says, "For this is the way God loved the world: He gave his one and only Son, so that everyone who believes in him will not perish but have eternal life" (John 3:16).

OUR SIN SEPARATES US FROM GOD

We are all sinners by nature and by choice, and because of this we are separated from God, who is holy. God's Word says, "for all have sinned and fall short of the glory of God" (Romans 3:23).

JESUS DIED SO YOU MIGHT HAVE LIFE

The consequence of sin is death, but God's free gift of salvation is available to us. Jesus took the penalty for our sin when He died on the cross.

God's Word says, "For the payoff of sin is death, but the gift of God is eternal life in Christ Jesus our Lord" (Romans 6:23); "But God demonstrates his own love for us, in that while we were still sinners, Christ died for us" (Romans 5:8).

JESUS LIVES!

Death could not hold Him, and three days after His body was placed in the tomb Jesus rose again, defeating sin and death forever. He lives today in heaven and is preparing a place in eternity for all who believe in Him.

Jesus says, "There are many dwelling places in my Father's house. Otherwise, I would have told you, because I am going away to make ready a place for you. And if I go and make ready a place for you, I will come again and take you to be with me, so that where I am you may be too" (John 14:2–3).

KNOW YOU CAN BE FORGIVEN

Accepting Jesus as your Savior is not about what you can do, but rather about having faith in what Jesus has already done. It takes recognizing that you are a sinner, believing that Jesus died for your sins, and asking for forgiveness by placing your full trust in Jesus' work on the cross on your behalf.

God's Word says, "if you confess with your mouth that Jesus is Lord and believe in your heart that God raised him from the dead, you will be saved. For with the heart one believes and thus has righteousness and with the mouth one confesses and thus has salvation" (Romans 10:9–10).

ACCEPT CHRIST'S FREE GIFT OF SALVATION

Practically, what does that look like? With a sincere heart, you can pray a simple prayer like this:

Jesus,
I know that I am a sinner. I don't want to live another day without embracing the love and forgiveness that You have for me. I ask for Your forgiveness. I believe that You died for my sins and rose from the dead. I surrender all that I am and ask You to be Lord of my life. Help me to turn from my sin and follow You. Teach me what it means to walk in freedom as I live under Your grace, and help me to grow in Your ways as I seek to know You more. Amen.

CONNECT AND GROW

If you just prayed this prayer (or something similar in your own words) we'd love to connect with you!

You can email us at info@lovegodgreatly.com. We'd love to celebrate with you, pray with you, and help you connect to a local church. We are here to encourage you as you begin your new life as a child of God.

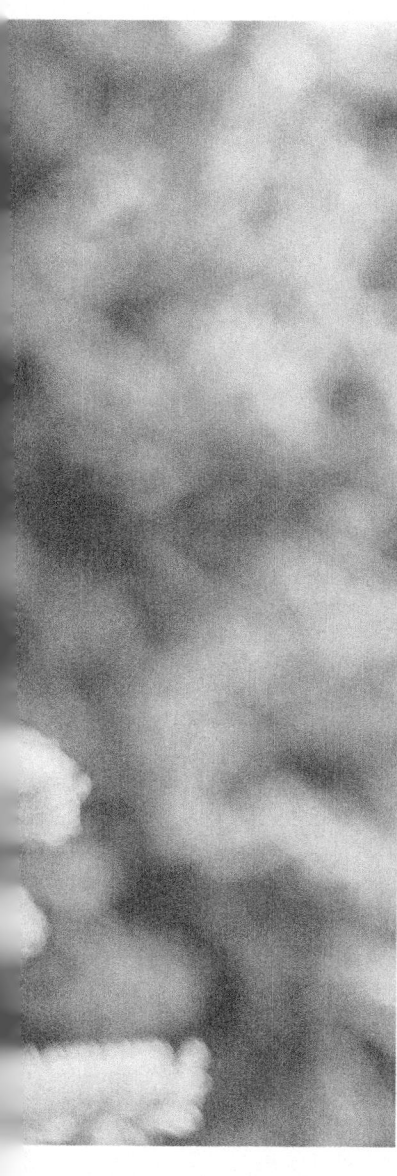

Let's Begin

REJOICE

Introduction

The word "Advent" is derived from Latin and means "coming" or "arrival." It's the four weeks leading up to Christmas when we remember the coming of Jesus. When we read the stories of Jesus' birth found in the pages of the gospel of Luke, we get a glimpse of what it was like for the people who first witnessed the arrival of the Messiah.

For 400 years after the prophet Malachi in the Old Testament, God did not speak to the Jewish people by sending new prophets. Some people wondered if God had withdrawn completely. Yet, all the God-fearing Jews in Israel were waiting for God's promised deliverer to come. It was a time of great expectation. *With the angel's announcement that the Messiah, the anointed One, was now about to arrive, there was great rejoicing among those who received the message.*

We will read of this rejoicing through people like Zechariah, who was filled with the Holy Spirit and burst into praise. His song is recorded in Luke 1:68-79 and also goes by the Latin name of "Benedictus." We will look at Simeon's joyful words (the "Nunc Dimittis") when he is allowed to see the infant Jesus, written in Luke 2:29-32. Mary also sings a beautiful song called the "Magnificat," in which she magnifies God, His character, and His deeds in her own life and throughout history (Luke 1:46-55). Not even the angels can contain their amazement when they announce the good news to the shepherds. Their joyful chorus called "Gloria in Excelsis" is recorded in Luke 2:14.

As we spend the next four weeks preparing our hearts for Christmas, let's pray that God will speak to us through His Word. Let's ask Him to help us grow in the knowledge of His glory, a glory which Zechariah, Simeon, Mary, the angels, and even the shepherds saw unfold in the coming of Jesus Christ. It is a glory which shines so brightly through these songs and leads us to rejoice this Advent season.

READING PLAN

WEEK 1 / ZECHARIAH'S SONG

- *Monday / Praise Out of Silence*
  Read: Luke 1:5-25; Luke 1:57-68
  SOAP: Luke 1:68

- *Tuesday / The Horn of Salvation*
  Read: Luke 1:68-75; Psalm 92:9-10; Colossians 1:11
  SOAP: Luke 1:69

- *Wednesday / Salvation from Our Enemies*
  Read: Luke 1:68-75; Zechariah 3:1-4; Hebrews 2:14-18
  SOAP: Luke 1:74

- *Thursday / John's Ministry*
  Read: Luke 1:76-77; John 1:19-37; John 3:22-30
  SOAP: John 3:27

- *Friday / God's Tender Mercy*
  Read: Luke 1:76-79; Mark 1:40-45; Hebrews 4:14-16
  SOAP: Luke 1:78-79

WEEK 2 / SIMEON'S SONG

- *Monday / The Restoration*
  Read: Luke 2:25-32; Isaiah 61:1-3; Psalm 147:1-3
  SOAP: Psalm 147:3

- *Tuesday / God's Word and God's Spirit*
  Read: Luke 2:21-26; John 14:15-26
  SOAP: John 14:26

- *Wednesday / My Eyes Have Seen Your Salvation*
  Read: Luke 2:28-32; Psalm 34:4-8; Hebrews 12:1-3
  SOAP: Luke 2:28-30

- *Thursday / Light of the World*
  Read: Luke 2:28-32; Isaiah 42:1-9; John 1:4-5
  SOAP: Luke 2:30-32

- *Friday / Child of Destiny*
  Read: Luke 2:28-35; Isaiah 8:14-15; John 3:18-21
  SOAP: Luke 2:34-35

WEEK 3 / MARY'S SONG

- ○ *Monday / Mary's Joy*
  Read: Luke 1:26-56; 1 Peter 1:3-12
  SOAP: Luke 1:46-47

- ○ *Tuesday / Holy is His Name*
  Read: Luke 1:46-49; Matthew 11:25-30; 1 Corinthians 1:18-31
  SOAP: Luke 1:48-49

- ○ *Wednesday / The Fear of God*
  Read: Luke 1:49-50; Luke 12:1-8; Hebrews 12:25-29
  SOAP: Luke 1:50

- ○ *Thursday / God Opposes the Proud*
  Read: Luke 1:51-53; Revelation 3:17-20; James 4:6-10
  SOAP: Luke 1:52-53

- ○ *Friday / The God Who Remembers*
  Read: Luke 1:54-55; Genesis 15:1-21; Matthew 26:27-28
  SOAP: Luke 1:54-55

WEEK 4 / THE ANGELS' SONG

- ○ *Monday / Glory and Poverty*
  Read: Luke 2:1-20; 2 Corinthians 8:9; Philippians 2:5-11
  SOAP: 2 Corinthians 8:9

- ○ *Tuesday / Why Angels Sang*
  Read: Luke 2:13-14; 1 Peter 1:10-12; Revelation 5:6-14
  SOAP: Luke 2:13

- ○ *Wednesday / Glory to God*
  Read: Luke 2:9-14; John 1:14; Hebrews 1:1-3
  SOAP: John 1:14

- ○ *Thursday / Peace on Earth*
  Read: Luke 2:14; Isaiah 9:6; Romans 5:1-11
  SOAP: Luke 2:14

- ○ *Friday / The Song of the Shepherds*
  Read: Luke 2:15-20; Philippians 2:9-11; Revelation 15:1-4
  SOAP: Philippians 2:9-11

YOUR GOALS

Write three goals you would like to focus on as you begin each day and dig into God's Word. Make sure you refer back to these goals throughout the next weeks to help you stay focused. You can do it!

ONE

....
....
....
....
....
....
....

TWO

....
....
....
....
....
....
....

THREE

....
....
....
....
....
....
....

WEEK 1

"*Blessed* be the <u>Lord God</u> of Israel, because he has come to <u>help</u> and has <u>redeemed</u> his people."

Luke 1:68

PRAY

Write down your prayer requests and praises for this week.

WEEKLY CHALLENGE

As we enter the Advent season, what practical steps can you take to have enough time of quiet and stillness for prayer and Bible study? Very often, this is one of the busiest times of the year. It can be challenging to keep our priorities right. Ask God for specific help in this. One way to spend time in God's Word is by memorizing Mary's in Luke 1:46-55, also known as the Magnificat. This week, begin memorizing Luke 1:46-48.

WEEK 1
Monday

READ

Luke 1:5-25

During the reign of Herod king of Judea, there lived a priest named Zechariah who belonged to the priestly division of Abijah, and he had a wife named Elizabeth, who was a descendant of Aaron. 6 They were both righteous in the sight of God, following all the commandments and ordinances of the Lord blamelessly. 7 But they did not have a child because Elizabeth was barren, and they were both very old. 8 Now while Zechariah was serving as priest before God when his division was on duty, 9 he was chosen by lot, according to the custom of the priesthood, to enter the Holy Place of the Lord and burn incense. 10 Now the whole crowd of people were praying outside at the hour of the incense offering. 11 An angel of the Lord, standing on the right side of the altar of incense, appeared to him. 12 And Zechariah, visibly shaken when he saw the angel, was seized with fear. 13 But the angel said to him, "Do not be afraid, Zechariah, for your prayer has been heard, and your wife Elizabeth will bear you a son; you will name him John. 14 Joy and gladness will come to you, and many will rejoice at his birth, 15 for he will be great in the sight of the Lord. He must never drink wine or strong drink, and he will be filled with the Holy Spirit, even before his birth. 16 He will turn many of the people of Israel to the Lord their God. 17 And he will go as forerunner before the Lord in the

> **WEEK 1**
> *Monday*

Luke 1:5-25 (continued)

spirit and power of Elijah, to turn the hearts of the fathers back to their children and the disobedient to the wisdom of the just, to make ready for the Lord a people prepared for him." 18 Zechariah said to the angel, "How can I be sure of this? For I am an old man, and my wife is old as well." 19 The angel answered him, "I am Gabriel, who stands in the presence of God, and I was sent to speak to you and to bring you this good news. 20 And now because you did not believe my words, which will be fulfilled in their time, you will be silent, unable to speak, until the day these things take place." 21 Now the people were waiting for Zechariah, and they began to wonder why he was delayed in the Holy Place. 22 When he came out, he was not able to speak to them. They realized that he had seen a vision in the Holy Place because he was making signs to them and remained unable to speak. 23 When his time of service was over, he went to his home. 24 After some time his wife Elizabeth became pregnant, and for five months she kept herself in seclusion. She said, 25 "This is what the Lord has done for me at the time when he has been gracious to me, to take away my disgrace among people."

WEEK 1

Monday

Luke 1:57-68

Now the time came for Elizabeth to have her baby, and she gave birth to a son. 58 Her neighbors and relatives heard that the Lord had shown great mercy to her, and they rejoiced with her. 59 On the eighth day they came to circumcise the child, and they wanted to name him Zechariah after his father. 60 But his mother replied, "No! He must be named John." 61 They said to her, "But none of your relatives bears this name." 62 So they made signs to the baby's father, inquiring what he wanted to name his son. 63 He asked for a writing tablet and wrote, "His name is John." And they were all amazed. 64 Immediately Zechariah's mouth was opened and his tongue released, and he spoke, blessing God. 65 All their neighbors were filled with fear, and throughout the entire hill country of Judea all these things were talked about. 66 All who heard these things kept them in their hearts, saying, "What then will this child be?" For the Lord's hand was indeed with him. 67 Then his father Zechariah was filled with the Holy Spirit and prophesied, 68 "Blessed be the Lord God of Israel, because he has come to help and has redeemed his people.

SOAP
WEEK 1 · MONDAY

SOAP / *Luke 1:68*
SCRIPTURE / *Write out the SOAP verses*

OBSERVATION / *Write 3 - 4 observations*

APPLICATION / *Write down 1 - 2 applications*

PRAYER / *Write out a prayer over what you learned*

DEVOTION
WEEK 1 • MONDAY

SOAP

Luke 1:68

"*Blessed be the Lord God of Israel, because he has come to help and has redeemed his people.*"

INTO THE TEXT

Zechariah spent more than nine months in silence. God had rebuked him for his unbelief of the angel's words that his wife Elizabeth would finally have a son after many years of infertility, longing, praying, and waiting. Because he did not believe, Zechariah had to spend many days not being able to talk to his family and friends. This gave him ample time to think, to be quiet, and to reflect on God's words.

As we start another Advent season we need to ask ourselves: Do we have enough time to be quiet before God? If we want to meet with God and be filled with the Holy Spirit, it is vital that we spend time in prayer and meditate on God's Words. We are surrounded by so much noise that it often takes great discipline and a firm resolve to switch off the TV, put away our phones, go into our room, close the door and - in that stillness - spend time alone with God.

In today's passage, we can see that the long months of stillness had been good for Zechariah. His first words after the birth of his son were that of praise to God as he was filled with the Holy Spirit. He even prophesied about the amazing events that were about to take place. Even though God had rebuked and punished him for his lack of faith, Zechariah had not grown bitter or angry. He now believed every word which Gabriel had spoken to him and was filled with deep thankfulness that the long-awaited Messiah was about to appear.

In our own lives, there are two very different responses we can have to the difficulties and trials God sends our way. We can either harden our hearts, become bitter, and shake our fists at God for allowing such suffering, or we can choose to trust Him in the midst of the darkness. We can believe in His words and His ways even when we can't understand them. God often uses difficulties to humble us and to draw us nearer to Himself. Let's trust Him, even in the dark times. He has promised to work them out for our good.

PRAYER

Lord Jesus, draw me closer to you even through my trials. Help me to be still before you. Amen.

WEEK 1

Tuesday

READ

Luke 1:68-75

"Blessed be the Lord God of Israel, because he has come to help and has redeemed his people. 69 For he has raised up a horn of salvation for us in the house of his servant David, 70 as he spoke through the mouth of his holy prophets from long ago, 71 that we should be saved from our enemies and from the hand of all who hate us. 72 He has done this to show mercy to our ancestors, and to remember his holy covenant— 73 the oath that he swore to our ancestor Abraham. This oath grants 74 that we, being rescued from the hand of our enemies, may serve him without fear, 75 in holiness and righteousness before him for as long as we live.

Psalm 92:9-10

Indeed, look at your enemies, O Lord. Indeed, look at how your enemies perish. All the evildoers are scattered. 10 You exalt my horn like that of a wild ox. I am covered with fresh oil.

Colossians 1:11

being strengthened with all power according to his glorious might for the display of all patience and steadfastness, joyfully

SOAP

WEEK 1 · TUESDAY

SOAP / *Luke 1:69*
SCRIPTURE / *Write out the SOAP verses*

OBSERVATION / *Write 3 - 4 observations*

APPLICATION / *Write down 1 - 2 applications*

PRAYER / *Write out a prayer over what you learned*

DEVOTION
WEEK 1 • TUESDAY

SOAP

Luke 1:69

*"For he has raised up a horn of salvation for us
in the house of his servant David,"*

INTO THE TEXT

For centuries, the nation of Israel had been oppressed by foreign powers. The Assyrians, Babylonians, Persians, and Greeks had ruled over them. Now, they were under the heavy hand of Rome with its governors, laws, and high taxes. The Jewish people were longing for the Messiah to finally come and redeem them from these powerful intruders. He would have to be strong and mighty in order to accomplish that.

As Zechariah was filled with the Holy Spirit, he prophesied about the salvation the Messiah would bring. He knew the words of the prophets that God would send a deliverer from the house of David. Zechariah called Him the "Horn of Salvation."

In different places in the Old Testament, "horn" refers to the deadly weapon of the wild ox. If you have ever seen a full-grown ox with its massive horns, you will understand how in ancient times the horn was a sign of great strength and victory over the enemies. Zechariah understood that the Messiah who was about to come was strong and powerful and would secure victory for His people.

Sadly, Jesus was rejected by most of the people in Israel. He was not the earthly powerful king they had envisaged Messiah to be. Many people today still reject Jesus as weak and pathetic, someone who didn't fight back but instead was killed by His enemies. Yet, as Christians, we know that Jesus is strong. He was the only one able to live a life of victory over sin and the devil. He was strong enough to endure God's wrath on the cross. In His strength, He lifted every heavy bolder of our sins on Himself and walked through death where he was then raised to life in great power.

With the arrival of Jesus, God's power has broken into our world. He is the risen Lord. He lives. He is here. He is with us, and He is our strength. In faith, we can connect our weak lives to His mighty power, counting on His help and experiencing Jesus as the Horn of our Salvation.

PRAYER

Lord, I am weak but you are strong. Please strengthen me according to your glorious power so that I can overcome sin and do what you want me to do. Amen.

WEEK 1
Wednesday

READ

Luke 1:68-75

"Blessed be the Lord God of Israel, because he has come to help and has redeemed his people. 69 For he has raised up a horn of salvation for us in the house of his servant David, 70 as he spoke through the mouth of his holy prophets from long ago, 71 that we should be saved from our enemies and from the hand of all who hate us. 72 He has done this to show mercy to our ancestors, and to remember his holy covenant— 73 the oath that he swore to our ancestor Abraham. This oath grants 74 that we, being rescued from the hand of our enemies, may serve him without fear, 75 in holiness and righteousness before him for as long as we live.

Zechariah 3:1-4

Next I saw Joshua the high priest standing before the angel of the Lord, with Satan standing at his right hand to accuse him. 2 The Lord said to Satan, "May the Lord rebuke you, Satan! May the Lord, who has chosen Jerusalem, rebuke you! Isn't this man like a burning stick snatched from the fire?" 3 Now Joshua was dressed in filthy clothes as he stood there before the angel. 4 The angel spoke up to those standing all around, "Remove his filthy clothes." Then he said to Joshua, "I have freely forgiven your iniquity and will dress you in fine clothing."

Hebrews 2:14-18

Therefore, since the children share in flesh and blood, he likewise shared in their humanity, so that through death he could destroy the one who holds the power of death (that is, the devil), 15 and set free those who were held in slavery all their lives by their fear of death. 16 For surely his concern is not for angels, but he is concerned for Abraham's descendants. 17 Therefore he had to be made like his brothers and sisters in every respect, so that he could become a merciful and faithful high priest in things relating to God, to make atonement for the sins of the people. 18 For since he himself suffered when he was tempted, he is able to help those who are tempted.

SOAP

WEEK 1 • WEDNESDAY

SOAP / *Luke 1:74*
SCRIPTURE / *Write out the SOAP verses*

OBSERVATION / *Write 3 - 4 observations*

APPLICATION / *Write down 1 - 2 applications*

PRAYER / *Write out a prayer over what you learned*

DEVOTION
WEEK 1 • WEDNESDAY

SOAP

Luke 1:74

"that we, being rescued from the hand of our enemies, may serve him without fear,"

INTO THE TEXT

Zechariah was a faithful Jew who believed all the covenant promises made by God in the Old Testament. He knew that the Messiah was coming to rescue His people from their enemies. What he did not yet understand was that the redemption which Jesus would bring at his first coming was not from the Romans or any other human government. He was coming to deliver His people from their real enemies: Satan, sin, and death.

When Satan was tempting Jesus in the desert, showing him all the kingdoms of the world and proclaiming that he was their owner, Jesus did not contradict him. Paul speaks of the devil as the "god of this age" (2 Corinthians 4:4). We have all felt something of the devil's evil rule in our own lives, families, and societies. Even when people want to be honest, loving, caring, and able to break free from the power of darkness, they can't. We can't due to our sinful nature and the enemy's influence. We need a Savior, a Rescuer.

How did Jesus redeem us from the power of Satan? He came to deal with our sin. By carrying it to the cross, Jesus has removed it forever. Being unable to accuse, Satan has now lost his power over those who come to Jesus for refuge. We are safe and secure in the arms of Christ when we place our faith in Him. God has "delivered us from the power of darkness and transferred us to the kingdom of the Son he loves, in whom we have redemption, the forgiveness of sins." (Colossians 1:13-14)

Jesus not only forgives those who trust in Him, but changes us, giving us the power to live righteous lives. We ourselves can't break the chains of our selfishness, bad attitudes, or destructive behavior, but Jesus can. He is strong enough to free us from anything that still holds us in bondage. When we go to him in faith and ask Him for forgiveness and deliverance from sin, He will answer. He wants to fill us with His love so that we can live fully surrendered to His will and way as well as live selflessly for other people. Our enemy trembles when we pray like this.

As Zechariah sings, Jesus has come to redeem us so that we can serve God in holiness.

PRAYER

Lord Jesus, thank you for dealing with my sin by carrying it to the cross. Thank you for forgiving me, for delivering me, and for continuing your work of sanctification in me. Amen.

WEEK 1
Thursday

READ

Luke 1:76-77

And you, child, will be called the prophet of the Most High. For you will go before the Lord to prepare his ways, 77 to give his people knowledge of salvation through the forgiveness of their sins.

John 3:22-30

After this, Jesus and his disciples came into Judean territory, and there he spent time with them and was baptizing. 23 John was also baptizing at Aenon near Salim because water was plentiful there, and people were coming to him and being baptized. 24 (For John had not yet been thrown into prison.) 25 Now a dispute came about between some of John's disciples and a certain Jew concerning ceremonial washing. 26 So they came to John and said to him, "Rabbi, the one who was with you on the other side of the Jordan River, about whom you testified—see, he is baptizing, and everyone is flocking to him!" 27 John replied, "No one can receive anything unless it has been given to him from heaven. 28 You yourselves can testify that I said, 'I am not the Christ,' but rather, 'I have been sent before him.' 29 The one who has the bride is the bridegroom. The friend of the bridegroom, who stands by and listens for him, rejoices greatly when he hears the bridegroom's voice. This then is my joy, and it is complete. 30 He must become more important while I become less important."

WEEK 1
Thursday

John 1:19-37

Now this was John's testimony when the Jewish leaders sent priests and Levites from Jerusalem to ask him, "Who are you?" 20 He confessed—he did not deny but confessed—"I am not the Christ!" 21 So they asked him, "Then who are you? Are you Elijah?" He said, "I am not!" "Are you the Prophet?" He answered, "No!" 22 Then they said to him, "Who are you? Tell us so that we can give an answer to those who sent us. What do you say about yourself?" 23 John said, "I am **the voice of one shouting in the wilderness, 'Make straight the way for the Lord,'** as the prophet Isaiah said." 24 (Now they had been sent from the Pharisees.) 25 So they asked John, "Why then are you baptizing if you are not the Christ, nor Elijah, nor the Prophet?" 26 John answered them, "I baptize with water. Among you stands one whom you do not recognize, 27 who is coming after me. I am not worthy to untie the strap of his sandal!" 28 These things happened in Bethany across the Jordan River where John was baptizing. 29 On the next day John saw Jesus coming toward him and said, "Look, the Lamb of God who takes away the sin of the world! 30 This is the one about whom I said, 'After me comes a man who is greater than I am, because he existed before me.' 31 I did not recognize him, but I came baptizing with water so that he could be revealed to Israel." 32 Then John testified, "I saw the Spirit descending like a dove from heaven, and it remained on him. 33 And I did not recognize him, but the one who sent me to baptize with water said to me, 'The one on whom you see the Spirit descending and remaining—this is the one who baptizes with the Holy Spirit.' 34 I have both seen and testified that this man is the Chosen One of God." 35 Again the next day John was standing there with two of his disciples. 36 Gazing at Jesus as he walked by, he said, "Look, the Lamb of God!" 37 When John's two disciples heard him say this, they followed Jesus.

Let's trust Him, even in the dark times. He has promised to work them out for our good.

SOAP

WEEK 1 · THURSDAY

SOAP / *John 3:27*
SCRIPTURE / *Write out the SOAP verses*

OBSERVATION / *Write 3 - 4 observations*

APPLICATION / *Write down 1 - 2 applications*

PRAYER / *Write out a prayer over what you learned*

DEVOTION
WEEK 1 · THURSDAY

SOAP

John 3:27

"John replied, "No one can receive anything unless it has been given to him from heaven."

INTO THE TEXT

Zechariah rightly understood that his son was not the promised king. When he praised God in song, he did it in front of all those gathered for the circumcision of his own son, John. And yet, most of his song was about the coming of Jesus. It was only in two verses that Zechariah actually mentions his son's ministry. He repeated what the angel had said John would do: he was going to be the promised forerunner to the Messiah, preparing people's hearts for the actual King.

We see in John's ministry later on that he was faithful to God's calling. Even though he was well known in all of Israel, respected and with a large following, he made sure to tell his listeners that he was not the Messiah. He said that Jesus was so much greater than him that he was not even worthy to untie His sandals.

John's testimony was so effective that most people - even some of his own disciples - gradually left him, gathering around Jesus instead. While he had once been surrounded by large crowds, life became more and more quiet for John. Eventually, he would end up in prison, alone and forgotten by most.

Was John's life a failure? Not at all. He had pointed people to Jesus. He had learned what it meant to die to himself, his popularity, his influence, and his ambitions in order to glorify Jesus. The only thing that counted for him was to fulfill God's calling on his life, even if that meant fading away into obscurity.

It's good to remember that it is God who decides what ministry He will give to each of His children. We need to let Him show us where He wants us to serve Him. If we're honest, it's not easy to say "yes, Lord" when He only gives us a small ministry, especially when we have something so much "bigger" and "more important" in mind. There may even be times when we wonder if God has forgotten about us. Even in those difficult moments, let's not forget that "dying to self" is part of God's purifying work in His children. In the end, a life of making Jesus greater than ourselves is more fruitful and fulfilling than anything else.

PRAYER

Jesus, you know how often I seek my own honor rather than yours. Please forgive me and help me to live for your glory alone. Amen.

WEEK 1
Friday

READ

Luke 1:76-79

And you, child, will be called the prophet of the Most High. For you will go before the Lord to prepare his ways, 77 to give his people knowledge of salvation through the forgiveness of their sins. 78 Because of our God's tender mercy, the dawn will break upon us from on high 79 to give light to those who sit in darkness and in the shadow of death, to guide our feet into the way of peace."

Hebrews 4:14-16

Therefore since we have a great high priest who has passed through the heavens, Jesus the Son of God, let us hold fast to our confession. 15 For we do not have a high priest incapable of sympathizing with our weaknesses, but one who has been tempted in every way just as we are, yet without sin. 16 Therefore let us confidently approach the throne of grace to receive mercy and find grace whenever we need help.

Mark 1:40-45

Now a leper came to him and fell to his knees, asking for help. "If you are willing, you can make me clean," he said. 41 Moved with indignation, Jesus stretched out his hand and touched him, saying, "I am willing. Be clean!" 42 The leprosy left him at once, and he was clean. 43 Immediately Jesus sent the man away with a very strong warning. 44 He told him, "See that you do not say anything to anyone, but go, show yourself to a priest, and bring the offering that Moses commanded for your cleansing, as a testimony to them." 45 But as the man went out he began to announce it publicly and spread the story widely, so that Jesus was no longer able to enter any town openly but stayed outside in remote places. Still they kept coming to him from everywhere.

SOAP

WEEK 1 · FRIDAY

SOAP / *Luke 1:78-79*
SCRIPTURE / *Write out the SOAP verses*

OBSERVATION / *Write 3 - 4 observations*

APPLICATION / *Write down 1 - 2 applications*

PRAYER / *Write out a prayer over what you learned*

DEVOTION
WEEK 1 · FRIDAY

SOAP

Luke 1:78-79

"Because of our God's tender mercy, the dawn will break upon us from on high to give light to those who sit in darkness and in the shadow of death, to guide our feet into the way of peace."

INTO THE TEXT

Zechariah beautifully described how God's tender mercy came down from heaven. Even though God is holy and all-powerful, He came to earth like the dawn. He didn't come with deadly energy, like a lightning flash, to crush us. Neither did He come like a meteorite, bright and spectacular, but destructive upon impact. In Jesus, God came like a gentle, quiet sunrise, a light hardly visible at first but gradually growing brighter and brighter until all the darkness of the night is swallowed up.

God came from heaven because He is merciful, meaning He is compassionate and feels great tenderness towards those He made. When He sees us in our sin and guilt, His heart is moved, and He wants to help us. He gave us His Son, who left the glory of heaven in order to be one of us and live on this earth. Instead of punishing us as we deserved, He allowed His own perfect Son to face our punishment, so we can be forgiven. God does not help us because of anything we have done, are doing now, or will do in the future. Instead, He does so out of His great mercy and love towards us.

When we look at Jesus in the Gospels, we can clearly see God's mercy. Even though Jesus was pure and without sin, He did not hesitate to receive sinners. He had long conversations with Pharisees, attended dinner parties with tax collectors, and called sinful men and women to follow Him. In the story we read today, Jesus didn't just say the words to heal a man with the dreaded disease of leprosy. In compassion, He stretched out His hand and touched him.

When God comes to us in Jesus, it is like the sunrise after a long and cold night. He comes near to us and doesn't draw away. He takes away the darkness of sin, fear, despair, and sorrow. The day will become brighter and brighter until we see Him in heaven, where we will live in His glorious, healing light forever. Let's join with Zechariah in praising our God who is so tender in mercy.

PRAYER

Heavenly Father, thank you for your tender mercy, sending your Son, and being so compassionate with me day after day. Help me become more merciful towards others. Amen.

REFLECT

WEEK 1

1. The Psalmist says: "Before I was afflicted I used to stray off, but now I keep your instructions...It was good for me to suffer so that I might learn your statutes." (Psalm 119:67, 71) Can you say the same? Have you ever been drawn closer to God through hardships? What did you learn about God's character during that time?

....
....
....

2. Jesus says: "My grace is enough for you, for my power is made perfect in weakness." (2 Corinthians 12:9) How have you experienced Jesus' power and strength in your own life through the salvation found in Him alone?

....
....
....

3. What tactics does Satan commonly use to distract, disengage, or deter you from daily walking with Christ? How can the truth of the Gospel help you fight the enemy's lies?

....
....
....

4. How are you allowing God to use you to serve His kingdom and accept whatever job He assigns to you? In what ways are you tempted to seek your own honor rather than that of Jesus?

....
....
....

5. In what areas of your life do you need help today? How can you go to Jesus confidently, knowing that He is merciful, and ask Him specifically for help?

....
....
....

JOURNAL

your thoughts

JOURNAL
your thoughts

WEEK 2

> "For my eyes have seen your salvation that you have prepared in the presence of all peoples"
>
> Luke 2:30-31

PRAY

Write down your prayer requests and praises for this week.

....
....
....
....
....
....
....
....
....
....
....
....

WEEKLY CHALLENGE

Advent is a time of waiting for Jesus' second coming when He will create a new earth and all our trials will finally be over. This week, we will think about Simeon, who had to wait for a long time to see Jesus the Messiah. Waiting is not easy for any of us. What are some of the things you have been waiting for? Commit them to God again this week, trusting in His perfect timing to answer your prayers. Also, continue memorizing Mary's song. Review what you memorized last week and begin memorizing Luke 1:49-50 this week.

....
....
....
....
....

WEEK 2
Monday

READ

Luke 2:25-32

Now there was a man in Jerusalem named Simeon who was righteous and devout, looking for the restoration of Israel, and the Holy Spirit was upon him. 26 It had been revealed to him by the Holy Spirit that he would not die before he had seen the Lord's Christ. 27 So Simeon, directed by the Spirit, came into the temple courts, and when the parents brought in the child Jesus to do for him what was customary according to the law, 28 Simeon took him in his arms and blessed God, saying, 29 "Now, according to your word, Sovereign Lord, permit your servant to depart in peace. 30 For my eyes have seen your salvation 31 that you have prepared in the presence of all peoples: 32 a light, for revelation to the Gentiles and for glory to your people Israel."

Psalm 147:1-3

Praise the Lord, for it is good to sing praises to our God. Yes, praise is pleasant and appropriate. 2 The Lord rebuilds Jerusalem and gathers the exiles of Israel. 3 He heals the brokenhearted and bandages their wounds.

Isaiah 61:1-3

The Spirit of the Sovereign Lord is upon me, because the Lord has chosen me. He has commissioned me to encourage the poor, to help the brokenhearted, to decree the release of captives and the freeing of prisoners, 2 to announce the year when the Lord will show his favor, the day when our God will seek vengeance, to console all who mourn, 3 to strengthen those who mourn in Zion by giving them a turban, instead of ashes, oil symbolizing joy, instead of mourning, a garment symbolizing praise, instead of discouragement. They will be called oaks of righteousness, trees planted by the Lord to reveal his splendor.

SOAP
WEEK 2 · MONDAY

SOAP / *Psalm 147:3*
SCRIPTURE / *Write out the SOAP verses*

OBSERVATION / *Write 3 - 4 observations*

APPLICATION / *Write down 1 - 2 applications*

PRAYER / *Write out a prayer over what you learned*

DEVOTION
WEEK 2 · MONDAY

SOAP

Psalm 147:3

"He heals the brokenhearted and bandages their wounds."

INTO THE TEXT

Many people in the Old Testament had been waiting for the Savior whom God would send into the world. He had announced it first in Genesis 3:15 and many more times through the following centuries. When Eve had her first son, she probably wondered if this was the promised one. Instead, Cain became the murderer of his brother Abel.

This anticipation and waiting continued throughout the history of God's people. The patriarch, Jacob, longed for this Savior. As he was dying, he cried out "I wait for your deliverance, O Lord" (Genesis 49:18). And the prophet Isaiah prayed impatiently, "If only you would tear apart the sky and come down" (Isaiah 64:1). Many had received God's Word about a coming deliverer and all died while waiting for the promised One.

All except for one: old Simeon. He, too, had waited many years for God's promise to be fulfilled. Imagine what his interactions with his friends were like: "Simeon, you always look like you're waiting for something. What is it?" "Oh yes, I'm waiting. Not for something but for someone. I'm waiting for the one who will bring restoration and comfort to our people."

Simeon was a man who knew that his people needed comfort. God showed him the condition of the human heart with its deep sadness, guilt, envy, pride, hunger for approval, fear of failure, and need for love - in one word: brokenness. Simeon knew that comfort and true restoring power could not be found in any person of earlier generations or anyone he had met during his life. But now, finally, he was allowed to see the one God had told him about. With deep joy, he held the baby, God's Son, in his arms and proclaimed: "My eyes have seen your salvation!"

What about us? We don't have to wait anymore. Jesus has come. We can simply open the door of our hearts and let Jesus in. Jesus, the comforter, the one who can heal our broken hearts, the one sent by God to bring us restoration, is with us now in our pain. He helps us day after day until we will one day see Him in heaven where we will not experience any sadness ever again.

PRAYER

Lord, you see my broken heart, you see my sadness, you know how much I need your comfort. Please restore to me the joy of your salvation. Amen.

WEEK 2
Tuesday

READ

Luke 2:21-26

At the end of eight days, when he was circumcised, he was named Jesus, the name given by the angel before he was conceived in the womb. 22 Now when the time came for their purification according to the law of Moses, Joseph and Mary brought Jesus up to Jerusalem to present him to the Lord 23 (just as it is written in the law of the Lord, "*Every firstborn male will be set apart to the Lord*"), 24 and to offer a sacrifice according to what is specified in the law of the Lord, **a pair of doves or two young pigeons.** 25 Now there was a man in Jerusalem named Simeon who was righteous and devout, looking for the restoration of Israel, and the Holy Spirit was upon him. 26 It had been revealed to him by the Holy Spirit that he would not die before he had seen the Lord's Christ.

John 14:15-26

"If you love me, you will obey my commandments. 16 Then I will ask the Father, and he will give you another Advocate to be with you forever— 17 the Spirit of truth, whom the world cannot accept because it does not see him or know him. But you know him because he resides with you and will be in you. 18 "I will not abandon you as orphans, I will come to you. 19 In a little while the world will not see me any longer, but you will see me; because I live, you will live too. 20 You will know at that time that I am in my Father and you are in me and I am in you. 21 The person who has my commandments and obeys them is the one who loves me. The one who loves me will be loved by my Father, and I will love him and will reveal myself to him." 22 "Lord," Judas (not Judas Iscariot) said, "what has happened that you are going to reveal yourself to us and not to the world?" 23 Jesus replied, "If anyone loves me, he will obey my word, and my Father will love him, and we will come to him and take up residence with him. 24 The person who does not love me does not obey my words. And the word you hear is not mine, but the Father's who sent me. 25 "I have spoken these things while staying with you. 26 But the Advocate, the Holy Spirit, whom the Father will send in my name, will teach you everything and will cause you to remember everything I said to you.

SOAP
WEEK 2 · TUESDAY

SOAP / *John 14:26*
SCRIPTURE / *Write out the SOAP verses*

OBSERVATION / *Write 3 - 4 observations*

APPLICATION / *Write down 1 - 2 applications*

PRAYER / *Write out a prayer over what you learned*

DEVOTION
WEEK 2 · TUESDAY

SOAP

John 14:26

"But the Advocate, the Holy Spirit, whom the Father will send in my name, will teach you everything and will cause you to remember everything I said to you."

INTO THE TEXT

Simeon was a living reminder to the people in Israel that they should not forget God's Words. Even though the promises of the coming Messiah had been made centuries before, Simeon did not doubt that God would come through. He knew deep in his heart that God does not lie and is always faithful to His promises. But there was something else which made Simeon so sure: the Holy Spirit had specifically revealed to him that he would not die before seeing the Messiah.

Simeon had two testimonies: the Word of God and the Holy Spirit. These are the same testimonies believers have today. Through the Word of God, the Bible, we learn of God's great deeds in redemptive history and His plans for the future. But only through the Holy Spirit can we truly understand these words and believe them personally.

It says in the Bible that God does not tolerate sin and will punish everyone for the wrong they have done. The Holy Spirit gives the specific warning, "YOU are under God's wrath!"

The Bible says to all people everywhere that God loved the world so much that He gave His Son. The Holy Spirit says, "It's for YOU that Jesus came."

The Bible points to the cross of Jesus and says, "Look, there is the lamb of God who carries away the sins of the world." The Holy Spirit speaks to our restless hearts and says, "Jesus took YOUR sins!"

It's amazing how God's Word and God's Spirit work together to bring us to faith in Jesus Christ. What do we need to do in order to believe? The answer is simple. Read the Bible and ask for the Holy Spirit to give you understanding. When we study the Bible without the help of God's Spirit, it will remain a dead book to us. And when we seek the Holy Spirit without the Bible, we quickly end up in all sorts of weird teachings and imaginations. God's Word and the Holy Spirit always belong together.

PRAYER

Lord, let your Word and your Spirit accomplish their powerful work in me. Amen.

WEEK 2
Wednesday

READ

Luke 2:28-32

Simeon took him in his arms and blessed God, saying, 29 "Now, according to your word, Sovereign Lord, permit your servant to depart in peace. 30 For my eyes have seen your salvation 31 that you have prepared in the presence of all peoples: 32 a light, for revelation to the Gentiles and for glory to your people Israel."

Psalm 34:4-8

I sought the Lord's help and he answered me; he delivered me from all my fears. 5 Look to him and be radiant; do not let your faces be ashamed. 6 This oppressed man cried out and the Lord heard; he saved him from all his troubles. 7 The angel of the Lord camps around the Lord's loyal followers and delivers them. 8 Taste and see that the Lord is good. How blessed is the one who takes shelter in him.

Hebrews 12:1-3

Therefore, since we are surrounded by such a great cloud of witnesses, we must get rid of every weight and the sin that clings so closely, and run with endurance the race set out for us, 2 keeping our eyes fixed on Jesus, the pioneer and perfecter of our faith. For the joy set out for him he endured the cross, disregarding its shame, and *has taken his seat at the right hand of the throne* of God. 3 Think of him who endured such opposition against himself by sinners, so that you may not grow weary in your souls and give up.

SOAP

WEEK 2 · WEDNESDAY

SOAP / *Luke 2:28-30*
SCRIPTURE / *Write out the SOAP verses*

OBSERVATION / *Write 3 - 4 observations*

APPLICATION / *Write down 1 - 2 applications*

PRAYER / *Write out a prayer over what you learned*

DEVOTION
WEEK 2 • WEDNESDAY

SOAP

Luke 2:28-30

"Simeon took him in his arms and blessed God, saying, "Now, according to your word, Sovereign Lord, permit your servant to depart in peace. For my eyes have seen your salvation"

INTO THE TEXT

It's an amazing scene. Simeon, an old man, took a little baby in his arms and broke into praise. He proclaimed that just by looking into the face of this child, he had seen God's salvation. Simeon never saw Jesus perform miracles or die on the cross and rise from the dead, yet he had seen enough just by looking at this tiny infant. He firmly believed that by seeing Jesus, He had seen God's salvation.

Simeon truly lived by faith. He simply accepted what God had told him. This is what faith is: being 100% sure that what God declares to be true is really true. We are certain of the things we cannot see with our physical eyes because we see them clearly with our inner, spiritual eyes. It is like seeing the invisible as clearly as if it was visible. We truly believe God's Words, and we know for certain that they describe reality.

While we live 2000 years after Jesus came into this world as a baby, and while we can't see Him now, the Bible encourages us to "look" to Him and to "fix our eyes" on Him. Psalm 34 tells us that those who look to Him are helped in such a complete way that they are full of joy. They are radiant. They will not be put to shame. This psalm also explains what it means to "look" to Jesus. It is taking shelter in Him, seeking His help, crying out to Him, and believing Him.

We are so quick to "look" to other people for help. We often tell friends about our problems before even telling Jesus about them. We run after people, looking for comfort, understanding, and love, forgetting that everything we need is in Jesus. He is our salvation, help, strength, wisdom, comfort, peace, cleansing, and restoration. Before we look anywhere else, let's look to Jesus. When we see Him, we have truly seen God's salvation.

PRAYER

Lord Jesus, I look to you. You are my salvation, my everything. Please help me run this race with perseverance and teach me to fix my eyes on you. Amen.

WEEK 2
Thursday

READ

Luke 2:28-32

Simeon took him in his arms and blessed God, saying, 29 "Now, according to your word, Sovereign Lord, permit your servant to depart in peace. 30 For my eyes have seen your salvation 31 that you have prepared in the presence of all peoples: 32 a light, for revelation to the Gentiles and for glory to your people Israel."

John 1:4-5

In him was life, and the life was the light of mankind. 5 And the light shines on in the darkness, but the darkness has not mastered it.

Isaiah 42:1-9

Here is my servant whom I support, my chosen one in whom I take pleasure. I have placed my Spirit on him; he will make just decrees for the nations. 2 He will not cry out or shout; he will not publicize himself in the streets. 3 A crushed reed he will not break, a dim wick he will not extinguish; he will faithfully make just decrees. 4 He will not grow dim or be crushed before establishing justice on the earth; the coastlands will wait in anticipation for his decrees." 5 This is what the true God, the Lord, says— the one who created the sky and stretched it out, the one who fashioned the earth and everything that lives on it, the one who gives breath to the people on it, and life to those who live on it: 6 "I, the Lord, officially commission you; I take hold of your hand. I protect you and make you a covenant mediator for people and a light to the nations, 7 to open blind eyes, to release prisoners from dungeons, those who live in darkness from prisons. 8 "I am the Lord! That is my name! I will not share my glory with anyone else or the praise due me with idols. 9 Look, my earlier predictive oracles have come to pass; now I announce new events. Before they begin to occur, I reveal them to you."

SOAP

WEEK 2 • THURSDAY

SOAP / *Luke 2:30-32*
SCRIPTURE / *Write out the SOAP verses*

OBSERVATION / *Write 3 - 4 observations*

APPLICATION / *Write down 1 - 2 applications*

PRAYER / *Write out a prayer over what you learned*

DEVOTION
WEEK 2 • THURSDAY

SOAP

Luke 2:30-32

"For my eyes have seen your salvation that you have prepared in the presence of all peoples: a light, for revelation to the Gentiles and for glory to your people Israel."

INTO THE TEXT

Simeon gives us a beautiful and true description of the baby in his arms. He is the light for the Gentiles, as prophesied by Isaiah about 600 years earlier. Simeon knew that with the coming of the Messiah, God's kingdom was going to be built beyond the people of Israel and expand to every corner of the world. God would call the Gentiles to Himself, those who had previously not belonged to His people.

Two thousand years later, we can only marvel at how these prophetic words of Isaiah and Simeon have been fulfilled. History has proven time and again that Jesus truly is the light of the world. Everywhere the gospel was carried, no matter how great the darkness, the good news of Jesus brought light and new life.

Think about Paul, spreading this light in the Greco-Roman world of the first century. The gospel brought people from idol worship to faith in the living God. Think about the first-century Christians who rescued and cared for unwanted infants left on the towns' rubbish heaps. The good news of Jesus changes everything.

In more recent times, think of missionaries like John Paton sailing to island tribes in the South Pacific, bringing the light of Jesus and ending the horrible killings and cannibalism. Think of Amy Carmichael traveling to India and rescuing countless little girls from a life of temple prostitution. Think of Mary Slessor going into Nigeria and working among the Okoyong tribes, preaching Jesus. With many coming to faith, this helped to end the widespread practice of killing newborn twins. Think of what is happening in the Muslim world today, with many thousands of people having their eyes opened to the truth of the gospel and leaving the oppressive darkness of Islam.

We sometimes forget what a life-changing power the gospel has proven to be, bringing an end to century-old darkness wherever people have turned to its bright and glorious light. Take some time to pick up a missionary biography and read some of these stories for yourself. Let's pray for this light to continue to spread to the unreached places in our world.

PRAYER

Heavenly Father, thank you for causing the bright light of the gospel to shine in my heart. I ask you to send more believers as missionaries to take this light to those who are still in darkness. Here I am. Use me in whatever way you want. Amen.

WEEK 2
Friday

READ

Luke 2:28-35

Simeon took him in his arms and blessed God, saying, 29 "Now, according to your word, Sovereign Lord, permit your servant to depart in peace. 30 For my eyes have seen your salvation 31 that you have prepared in the presence of all peoples: 32 a light, for revelation to the Gentiles and for glory to your people Israel." 33 So the child's father and mother were amazed at what was said about him. 34 Then Simeon blessed them and said to his mother Mary, "Listen carefully: This child is destined to be the cause of the falling and rising of many in Israel and to be a sign that will be rejected. 35 Indeed, as a result of him the thoughts of many hearts will be revealed—and a sword will pierce your own soul as well!"

John 3:18-21

The one who believes in him is not condemned. The one who does not believe has been condemned already, because he has not believed in the name of the one and only Son of God. 19 Now this is the basis for judging: that the light has come into the world and people loved the darkness rather than the light because their deeds were evil. 20 For everyone who does evil deeds hates the light and does not come to the light, so that their deeds will not be exposed. 21 But the one who practices the truth comes to the light, so that it may be plainly evident that his deeds have been done in God.

Isaiah 8:14-15

He will become a sanctuary, but a stone that makes a person trip and a rock that makes one stumble— to the two houses of Israel. He will become a trap and a snare to the residents of Jerusalem. 15 Many will stumble over the stone and the rock, and will fall and be seriously injured, and will be ensnared and captured."

SOAP

WEEK 2 · FRIDAY

SOAP / *Luke 2:34-35*
SCRIPTURE / *Write out the SOAP verses*

OBSERVATION / *Write 3 - 4 observations*

APPLICATION / *Write down 1 - 2 applications*

PRAYER / *Write out a prayer over what you learned*

DEVOTION
WEEK 2 • FRIDAY

SOAP

Luke 2:34-35

"Then Simeon blessed them and said to his mother Mary, "Listen carefully: This child is destined to be the cause of the falling and rising of many in Israel and to be a sign that will be rejected. Indeed, as a result of him the thoughts of many hearts will be revealed—and a sword will pierce your own soul as well!"

INTO THE TEXT

Simeon was a man who had lived for one purpose: seeing the Messiah. Now that he had seen Him, he was fully satisfied and ready to die. He had faithfully testified that Jesus is the Savior of the world. Mary and Joseph must have rejoiced at the wonderful things being prophesied about their son.

Yet, the Holy Spirit now spoke some hard words through Simeon, words that Mary and Joseph probably did not want to hear. Their child would be "the cause of the falling and rising of many." Just as Isaiah had prophesied, Jesus would be a sanctuary, a place of priceless refuge for some. For others, He would be a crushing stone. He would lift some up to become children of God, giving them eternal glory in heaven. Others would fall to eternal punishment and disaster due to their unbelief.

Jesus would also be "a sign that will be rejected." Throughout His life, He was violently opposed, contested, and even executed. Throughout history, Jesus' name has been hated and mocked. His followers have been ridiculed, persecuted, and killed.

Jesus is the great divider. He is the point at which a heart can be revealed. The answer to the question "What do you believe about Jesus Christ?" is the most important question a person can answer. It reveals who you really are and determines your eternal destiny. Those who do not have Jesus as Savior and Lord show that they do not belong to God.

What matters is not that we have "some" kind of faith. What matters is that we have the right kind of faith. Believing in a god, Krishna, Buddha, Allah, or some other higher power will not save us. But believing in Jesus, putting all our trust in Him as our sin-bearer and righteousness-provider will make us God's children. We will have a secure place in heaven. This is not a popular belief in our modern world, but it is the way God has chosen. The little baby in Simeon's arms truly is the child of destiny. Everything - really everything - depends on what we do with Him.

PRAYER

Lord Jesus, you are precious to me. Thank you for revealing yourself to me. Please help me to share about you courageously with others. Amen.

REFLECT

WEEK 2

1. When have you experienced Jesus as the comforter? How has He restored your broken heart in the past?

   ....
   ....
   ....

2. Why do we need the help of the Holy Spirit in order to understand the Bible? How have you seen the Holy Spirit illuminate God's Word in your life?

   ....
   ....
   ....

3. What is true faith? What does it mean for you to "fix [your] eyes on Jesus?"

   ....
   ....
   ....

4. Where is God asking you to take the message of the gospel, the good news of Jesus Christ?

   ....
   ....
   ....

5. Do you find it hard to tell others about Jesus being the only way to God? Why or why not? Why is it crucial to speak about Jesus being the way, the truth, and the life (John 14:6)?

   ....
   ....
   ....

JOURNAL
your thoughts

JOURNAL
your thoughts

WEEK 3

"And Mary said, My soul <u>exalts</u> the Lord, and my spirit has begun to <u>rejoice</u> in God my (Savior)

Luke 1:46-47

PRAY

Write down your prayer requests and praises for this week.

WEEKLY CHALLENGE

"If you look at the world, you'll be distressed. If you look within, you'll be depressed. If you look at God, you'll be at rest." (Corrie Ten Boom) Mary beautifully shows us in her song of praise that she could rest and even rejoice in God despite her difficult circumstances. As we study the Magnificat this week, try to think of specific things you can praise God for. Also, continue memorizing this passage. Review what you memorized the last two weeks and begin memorizing Luke 1:51-53 this week.

WEEK 3

Monday

READ

Luke 1:26-56

In the sixth month of Elizabeth's pregnancy, the angel Gabriel was sent by God to a town of Galilee called Nazareth, 27 to a virgin engaged to a man whose name was Joseph, a descendant of David, and the virgin's name was Mary. 28 The angel came to her and said, "Greetings, favored one, the Lord is with you!" 29 But she was greatly troubled by his words and began to wonder about the meaning of this greeting. 30 So the angel said to her, "Do not be afraid, Mary, for you have found favor with God! 31 Listen: You will become pregnant and give birth to a son, and you will name him Jesus. 32 He will be great and will be called the Son of the Most High, and the Lord God will give him the throne of his father David. 33 He will reign over the house of Jacob forever, and his kingdom will never end." 34 Mary said to the angel, "How will this be, since I have not been intimate with a man?" 35 The angel replied, "The Holy Spirit will come upon you, and the power of the Most High will overshadow you. Therefore the child to be born will be holy; he will be called the Son of God. 36 "And look, your relative Elizabeth has also become pregnant with a son in her old age—although she was called barren, she is now in her sixth month! 37 For nothing will be impossible with God." 38 So Mary said, "Yes, I am a servant of the Lord; let this happen to me according to your word." Then the angel departed from her. 39 In those days Mary got up and went hurriedly into the hill country, to a town

WEEK 3

Monday

Luke 1:26-56 (continued)

of Judah, 40 and entered Zechariah's house and greeted Elizabeth. 41 When Elizabeth heard Mary's greeting, the baby leaped in her womb, and Elizabeth was filled with the Holy Spirit. 42 She exclaimed with a loud voice, "Blessed are you among women, and blessed is the child in your womb! 43 And who am I that the mother of my Lord should come and visit me? 44 For the instant the sound of your greeting reached my ears, the baby in my womb leaped for joy. 45 And blessed is she who believed that what was spoken to her by the Lord would be fulfilled." 46 And Mary said, "My soul exalts the Lord, 47 and my spirit has begun to rejoice in God my Savior, 48 because he has looked upon the humble state of his servant. For from now on all generations will call me blessed, 49 because he who is mighty has done great things for me, and holy is his name; 50 from generation to generation he is merciful to those who fear him. 51 He has demonstrated power with his arm; he has scattered those whose pride wells up from the sheer arrogance of their hearts. 52 He has brought down the mighty from their thrones, and has lifted up those of lowly position; 53 he has filled the hungry with good things, and has sent the rich away empty. 54 He has helped his servant Israel, remembering his mercy, 55 as he promised to our ancestors, to Abraham and to his descendants forever." 56 So Mary stayed with Elizabeth about three months and then returned to her home.

WEEK 3
Monday

1 Peter 1:3-12

Blessed be the God and Father of our Lord Jesus Christ! By his great mercy he gave us new birth into a living hope through the resurrection of Jesus Christ from the dead, 4 that is, into an inheritance imperishable, undefiled, and unfading. It is reserved in heaven for you, 5 who by God's power are protected through faith for a salvation ready to be revealed in the last time. 6 This brings you great joy, although you may have to suffer for a short time in various trials. 7 Such trials show the proven character of your faith, which is much more valuable than gold—gold that is tested by fire, even though it is passing away—and will bring praise and glory and honor when Jesus Christ is revealed. 8 You have not seen him, but you love him. You do not see him now but you believe in him, and so you rejoice with an indescribable and glorious joy, 9 because you are attaining the goal of your faith—the salvation of your souls. 10 Concerning this salvation, the prophets who predicted the grace that would come to you searched and investigated carefully. 11 They probed into what person or time the Spirit of Christ within them was indicating when he testified beforehand about the sufferings appointed for Christ and his subsequent glory. 12 They were shown that they were serving not themselves but you, in regard to the things now announced to you through those who proclaimed the gospel to you by the Holy Spirit sent from heaven—things angels long to catch a glimpse of.

SOAP

WEEK 3 · MONDAY

SOAP / *Luke 1:46-47*
SCRIPTURE / *Write out the SOAP verses*

OBSERVATION / *Write 3 - 4 observations*

APPLICATION / *Write down 1 - 2 applications*

PRAYER / *Write out a prayer over what you learned*

DEVOTION
WEEK 3 • MONDAY

SOAP

Luke 1:46-47

"And Mary said, "My soul exalts the Lord, and my spirit has begun to rejoice in God my Savior,"

INTO THE TEXT

Mary had just been told by the angel that she was going to conceive a baby. She was young and unmarried, a virgin. It would have been a great scandal for her to become pregnant outside of marriage. Mary undoubtedly knew what this would mean for her. She would face public shame, becoming the talk of the town. And what would her fiancé Joseph do? Surprisingly, though, Mary did not moan but rejoiced in God! Why? What was there to sing about?

Mary's heart was full of joyful praise because she looked to God, the One she knew would be with her and help her. Being full of faith, she was able to see beyond her immediate, challenging circumstances and meditate, instead, on the great deeds of God, past, present, and future. Her spirit was not filled with worries, fears, and the trifles of life. Her spirit soared above as she fixed her eyes on God, her Savior, and what He had done for her.

Mary simply took God at His word. She was confident that God would bring about everything He had said through the angel: "Mary, the Lord is with you. You are highly favored. Don't be afraid. This child you are going to have will be called the Son of the Most High, and He will be a great king. Nothing is impossible with God."

It is a very liberating thing to have our minds filled with God and His awesome character and wonderful deeds. Our troubles become less significant when we remember that God will be with us through this short life and that we have a Savior who is bringing us to eternal glory. We need to take Him at His Word. The whole Bible is full of God's precious promises to us. He wants us to believe them. If we could only lift our eyes above life's present difficulties and look in faith to Jesus, the Savior, our hearts would soon join in with Mary's hope-filled song of praise.

PRAYER

Lord, let my mind be increasingly filled with you, your character, and your deeds. Amen.

WEEK 3

Tuesday

READ

Luke 1:46-49

And Mary said, "My soul exalts the Lord, 47 and my spirit has begun to rejoice in God my Savior, 48 because he has looked upon the humble state of his servant. For from now on all generations will call me blessed, 49 because he who is mighty has done great things for me, and holy is his name;

Matthew 11:25-30

At that time Jesus said, "I praise you, Father, Lord of heaven and earth, because you have hidden these things from the wise and intelligent, and have revealed them to little children. 26 Yes, Father, for this was your gracious will. 27 All things have been handed over to me by my Father. No one knows the Son except the Father, and no one knows the Father except the Son and anyone to whom the Son decides to reveal him. 28 Come to me, all you who are weary and burdened, and I will give you rest. 29 Take my yoke on you and learn from me because I am gentle and humble in heart, and you will find rest for your souls. 30 For my yoke is easy to bear, and my load is not hard to carry."

WEEK 3
Tuesday

1 Corinthians 1:18-31

For the message about the cross is foolishness to those who are perishing, but to us who are being saved it is the power of God. 19 For it is written, "***I will destroy the wisdom of the wise, and I will thwart the cleverness of the intelligent.***" 20 Where is the wise man? Where is the expert in the Mosaic law? Where is the debater of this age? Has God not made the wisdom of the world foolish? 21 For since in the wisdom of God the world by its wisdom did not know God, God was pleased to save those who believe by the foolishness of preaching. 22 For Jews demand miraculous signs and Greeks ask for wisdom, 23 but we preach about a crucified Christ, a stumbling block to Jews and foolishness to Gentiles. 24 But to those who are called, both Jews and Greeks, Christ is the power of God and the wisdom of God. 25 For the foolishness of God is wiser than human wisdom, and the weakness of God is stronger than human strength. 26 Think about the circumstances of your call, brothers and sisters. Not many were wise by human standards, not many were powerful, not many were born to a privileged position. 27 But God chose what the world thinks foolish to shame the wise, and God chose what the world thinks weak to shame the strong. 28 God chose what is low and despised in the world, what is regarded as nothing, to set aside what is regarded as something, 29 so that no one can boast in his presence. 30 He is the reason you have a relationship with Christ Jesus, who became for us wisdom from God, and righteousness and sanctification and redemption, 31 so that, as it is written, "***Let the one who boasts, boast in the Lord.***"

Jesus is our salvation, help, strength, wisdom, comfort, peace, cleansing, and restoration.

SOAP

WEEK 3 · TUESDAY

SOAP / *Luke 1:48-49*
SCRIPTURE / *Write out the SOAP verses*

OBSERVATION / *Write 3 - 4 observations*

APPLICATION / *Write down 1 - 2 applications*

PRAYER / *Write out a prayer over what you learned*

DEVOTION
WEEK 3 · TUESDAY

SOAP

Luke 1:48-49

"because he has looked upon the humble state of his servant. For from now on all generations will call me blessed, because he who is mighty has done great things for me, and holy is his name;"

INTO THE TEXT

Mary meditated on God's incredible might and holiness. God is exalted above everything, He is holy and is separated from what is ordinary.

When the Bible speaks of God's holiness, it refers to His greatness and His moral perfection. God is different from us in that His heart and will are perfectly good, right, and lovely. God doesn't lie to us or trick us. He is totally upright. God doesn't break His promises. He is totally faithful. God does not turn a blind eye to injustice. He is totally impartial and just. God is not stingy and mean. He is overflowing with love, mercy, generosity, and kindness. God is holy, meaning that He is high above us and in a class by Himself. He is totally and uniquely beautiful. He is of infinite value. Even all of these descriptions cannot fully describe the holiness of God.

Instead of being scared of this mighty, exalted, and holy God, Mary was captivated by His beauty and filled with joy in His presence. His greatness has not kept Him from doing great things for her. God could have chosen the daughter of the king or high priest to give birth to Jesus. He could have chosen a girl who was rich, beautiful, educated, and admired. But, unlike us, God is not impressed by these attributes. Mary herself says that she was of a "humble state", meaning she was probably a nobody in her community, overlooked by the important people, an insignificant servant. And yet, the holy God chose her, a peasant girl from Nazareth, to be the mother of the Messiah. Mary was amazed that God would be so great and yet see somebody as low as her.

Have you, like Mary, come to know how exalted and holy God is? Do you know how small and sinful you are in comparison, and how much mercy and grace He has poured on you through His Son, Jesus Christ? Think about it: the infinitely great and perfect God has chosen you to be His beloved daughter. He has lifted you out of your sin and depravity. He has promised you eternal glory in heaven by your faith in Jesus. You are highly valued and infinitely loved by Him. May we, like Mary, rejoice in God's holiness.

PRAYER

Lord Jesus, you are so high above me in greatness and purity, yet you love me. You are not only mighty, but you are also good. Holy God, I thank you. Amen.

WEEK 3
Wednesday

READ

Luke 1:49-50

because he who is mighty has done great things for me, and holy is his name; 50 from generation to generation he is merciful to those who fear him.

Luke 12:1-8

Meanwhile, when many thousands of the crowd had gathered so that they were trampling on one another, Jesus began to speak first to his disciples, "Be on your guard against the yeast of the Pharisees, which is hypocrisy. 2 Nothing is hidden that will not be revealed, and nothing is secret that will not be made known. 3 So then whatever you have said in the dark will be heard in the light, and what you have whispered in private rooms will be proclaimed from the housetops. 4 "I tell you, my friends, do not be afraid of those who kill the body, and after that have nothing more they can do. 5 But I will warn you whom you should fear: Fear the one who, after the killing, has authority to throw you into hell. Yes, I tell you, fear him! 6 Aren't five sparrows sold for two pennies? Yet not one of them is forgotten before God. 7 In fact, even the hairs on your head are all numbered. Do not be afraid; you are more valuable than many sparrows. 8 "I tell you, whoever acknowledges me before men, the Son of Man will also acknowledge before God's angels.

Hebrews 12:25-29

Take care not to refuse the one who is speaking! For if they did not escape when they refused the one who warned them on earth, how much less shall we, if we reject the one who warns from heaven? 26 Then his voice shook the earth, but now he has promised, "***I will once more shake not only the earth but heaven too.***" 27 Now this phrase "***once more***" indicates the removal of what is shaken, that is, of created things, so that what is unshaken may remain. 28 So since we are receiving an unshakable kingdom, let us give thanks, and through this let us offer worship pleasing to God in devotion and awe. 29 For our ***God is indeed a devouring fire.***

SOAP

WEEK 3 • WEDNESDAY

SOAP / *Luke 1:50*
SCRIPTURE / *Write out the SOAP verses*

OBSERVATION / *Write 3 - 4 observations*

APPLICATION / *Write down 1 - 2 applications*

PRAYER / *Write out a prayer over what you learned*

DEVOTION
WEEK 3 · WEDNESDAY

SOAP

Luke 1:50

"from generation to generation he is merciful to those who fear him."

INTO THE TEXT

Throughout her song, Mary displayed a deep reverence for God. Sadly, there is not much fear of God in our world. Many people just smile when they hear about God's commandments. In their minds, God, if he exists, would not be so fussy as to punish people for their disobedience. After all, nobody is perfect, and we are all just trying our best. Some would say, "We are really not that bad, and God is very understanding." There is much trust in people's goodness and a great downplaying of God's holiness.

Fearing God means deeply respecting Him and carefully listening to what He says. It means taking seriously His warnings about sin and hell. It means knowing that because God is holy, powerful, and just, we would face certain destruction if we lived in rebellion against Him. We can only fear God when we see what He is like. We can increasingly get to know Him through the Bible.

The more clearly we see God's holiness, the more we will develop a proper reverence for Him. We will also see ourselves and our sin more clearly in His light. This will cause us to grieve as we realize that we cannot stand before a just God in our own righteousness. Fear of God will produce humility and a sensitive heart.

Mary knew that this fearsome God was full of mercy and compassion when He saw people in their sin and desperation. And we know what Mary did not yet know. The only safe place from God's punishment is the cross, the place where Jesus, God Himself, was punished for our sins. This is where we go for forgiveness and refuge. Here, we are no longer afraid of God but instead rejoice in His mercy. God, in His kindness, has saved us from His own wrath. And, like Mary, we will lose our fear of other people, their opinions, and judgements, as we fear only God.

PRAYER

Heavenly Father, help me to fear you more and other people less. Amen.

WEEK 3
Thursday

READ

Luke 1:51-53

He has demonstrated power with his arm; he has scattered those whose pride wells up from the sheer arrogance of their hearts. 52 He has brought down the mighty from their thrones, and has lifted up those of lowly position; 53 he has filled the hungry with good things, and has sent the rich away empty.

James 4:6-10

But he gives greater grace. Therefore it says, "**God opposes the proud, but he gives grace to the humble.**" 7 So submit to God. But resist the devil and he will flee from you. 8 Draw near to God and he will draw near to you. Cleanse your hands, you sinners, and make your hearts pure, you double-minded. 9 Grieve, mourn, and weep. Turn your laughter into mourning and your joy into despair. 10 Humble yourselves before the Lord and he will exalt you.

Revelation 3:17-20

Because you say, "I am rich and have acquired great wealth, and need nothing," but do not realize that you are wretched, pitiful, poor, blind, and naked, 18 take my advice and buy gold from me refined by fire so you can become rich! Buy from me white clothing so you can be clothed and your shameful nakedness will not be exposed, and buy eye salve to put on your eyes so you can see! 19 All those I love, I rebuke and discipline. So be earnest and repent! 20 Listen! I am standing at the door and knocking! If anyone hears my voice and opens the door I will come into his home and share a meal with him, and he with me.

SOAP

WEEK 3 • THURSDAY

SOAP / *Luke 1:52-53*
SCRIPTURE / *Write out the SOAP verses*

OBSERVATION / *Write 3 - 4 observations*

APPLICATION / *Write down 1 - 2 applications*

PRAYER / *Write out a prayer over what you learned*

DEVOTION
WEEK 3 · THURSDAY

SOAP

Luke 1:52-53

"He has brought down the mighty from their thrones, and has lifted up those of lowly position; he has filled the hungry with good things, and has sent the rich away empty."

INTO THE TEXT

Mary focused on another aspect of God's character. She stated that God is against the proud, arrogant, and self-sufficient but helps the humble. She contrasted how God brings down the rich and mighty while lifting up the poor and hungry. This may lead you to ask the question: Does God favor certain people above others? Is God not merciful to everyone?

A picture may help us understand this. While Jesus was hanging on the cross, his blood flowed out of His body. This blood was the river of God's love flowing into the whole world. Yet, just as objects above cannot be reached by water flowing downwards, so God's love is not received by the proud and arrogant who do not see their need for His mercy and forgiveness. It seems that the more secure people feel in this world through their popularity, wealth, or power, the harder it is for them to see their desperate need for God.

Water flows down into the valleys and is absorbed by soft soil. In the same way, God's mercy is received by humble people, whose hearts have been softened by His Spirit and broken by the realization that they are sinful and utterly unable to save themselves or change themselves. It is these people that God delights to help, for they humbly admit their need for Him. They ask Him for mercy and give Him the glory when He pours His grace on them.

So often we think that we need more money, influence, and friends. We admire and look up to those who are above us in beauty and status. In these moments, it's especially important to remember that God, who has nobody above Himself, looks to the despised and humbled. We should daily strive for humility, delighting when we can serve others. Even if we are overlooked or even rejected, we can trust that God sees us. He is a God who stoops down in mercy towards the most undeserving, unloved, and unworthy people in order to pour His grace on them in a special way.

PRAYER

Lord Jesus, you have softened my proud heart. You have poured your love on me, and you deeply care for me. Without your mercy, there would be no hope for me. Thank you for your love and grace. Amen.

WEEK 3
Friday

READ

Luke 1:54-55

He has helped his servant Israel, remembering his mercy, 55 as he promised to our ancestors, to Abraham and to his descendants forever."

Genesis 15:1-21

After these things the Lord's message came to Abram in a vision: "Fear not, Abram! I am your shield and the one who will reward you in great abundance." 2 But Abram said, "O Sovereign Lord, what will you give me since I continue to be childless, and my heir is Eliezer of Damascus?" 3 Abram added, "Since you have not given me a descendant, then look, one born in my house will be my heir!" 4 But look, the Lord's message came to him: "This man will not be your heir, but instead a son who comes from your own body will be your heir." 5 The Lord took him outside and said, "Gaze into the sky and count the stars—if you are able to count them!" Then he said to him, "So will your descendants be." 6 Abram believed the Lord, and the Lord credited it as righteousness to him. 7 The Lord said to him, "I am the Lord who brought you out from Ur of the Chaldeans to give you this land to possess." 8 But Abram said, "O Sovereign Lord, by what can I know that I am to possess it?" 9 The Lord said to him, "Take for me a heifer, a goat, and a ram, each three years old, along with a dove and a young pigeon." 10 So Abram took all these for him and then cut them in two and placed each half opposite the

WEEK 3
Friday

Genesis 15:1-21 (continued)

other, but he did not cut the birds in half. 11 When birds of prey came down on the carcasses, Abram drove them away. 12 When the sun went down, Abram fell sound asleep, and great terror overwhelmed him. 13 Then the Lord said to Abram, "Know for certain that your descendants will be strangers in a foreign country. They will be enslaved and oppressed for 400 years. 14 But I will execute judgment on the nation that they will serve. Afterward they will come out with many possessions. 15 But as for you, you will go to your ancestors in peace and be buried at a good old age. 16 In the fourth generation your descendants will return here, for the sin of the Amorites has not yet reached its limit." 17 When the sun had gone down and it was dark, a smoking firepot with a flaming torch passed between the animal parts. 18 That day the Lord made a covenant with Abram: "To your descendants I give this land, from the river of Egypt to the great river, the Euphrates River— 19 the land of the Kenites, Kenizzites, Kadmonites, 20 Hittites, Perizzites, Rephaites, 21 Amorites, Canaanites, Girgashites, and Jebusites."

Matthew 26:27-28

And after taking the cup and giving thanks, he gave it to them, saying, "Drink from it, all of you, 28 for this is my blood, the blood of the covenant, that is poured out for many for the forgiveness of sins.

Think about it: the infinitely great and perfect God has chosen you to be His beloved daughter.

SOAP

WEEK 3 · FRIDAY

SOAP / *Luke 1:54-55*
SCRIPTURE / *Write out the SOAP verses*

OBSERVATION / *Write 3 - 4 observations*

APPLICATION / *Write down 1 - 2 applications*

PRAYER / *Write out a prayer over what you learned*

DEVOTION
WEEK 3 · FRIDAY

SOAP

Luke 1:54-55

"He has helped his servant Israel, remembering his mercy, as he promised to our ancestors, to Abraham and to his descendants forever."

INTO THE TEXT

At the end of her hymn, Mary sang of the God who mercifully remembered His promises of long ago. Many centuries earlier, God had made a promise to Abraham. Throughout Israel's history, God remembered, renewed, and acted on this covenant promise. It did not depend on Israel's faithfulness but on God's mercy. In fact, many times He fulfilled His promises despite their rebellion and disobedience. Through Jesus, God was about to make a new and better covenant, one which fulfilled the promises made to Abraham but surpassed them far beyond what Mary could have imagined.

God made a new covenant with His people through the death of His own beloved Son. If God kept His covenant with Abraham, which was just a shadow of the coming new one, how much more can we trust Him to keep the promises which Jesus bought with His own blood? Jesus made promises to forgive us, renew us, fill us with the Holy Spirit, always be with us, and bring us to our eternal homes in heaven.

God remembering His promises is a great source of comfort to His people. Even when we feel like a failure, God still loves us and will not reject us. He can not and will not break the covenant He made with us. He is as faithful to us as He has been to all of His children throughout all of history. He does not look at our failures but instead remembers Jesus' work on the cross. This is where our hearts can rest. God remembers His covenant.

As Mary says, when God mercifully remembers His people, He comes to help them. In our own lives, have we not known God to remember us? Many times He has taken care of our needs, comforted us in our sadness, liberated us from sin, and guided us in difficult decisions. Let's join in Mary's song of praise to our holy God, our merciful Savior, and our faithful promise-keeper.

PRAYER

Heavenly Father, complete the work you have started in me. Help me to remember that your character never changes. Amen.

REFLECT

WEEK 3

1. What circumstances in your life make it difficult for you to praise God? How can you learn from Mary's example of praise?

   ....
   ....
   ....

2. How does it make you feel to know that God is holy? Are you thankful for His attributes and for the fact that He is so different from us?

   ....
   ....
   ....

3. As Christians, we don't have to be afraid of God anymore, but we should still fear Him. How would you explain the difference between fearing God according to Scripture and fearing someone according to the world's definition?

   ....
   ....
   ....

4. Why does Jesus say: "Blessed are the poor in spirit, for the kingdom of heaven belongs to them"? How can you begin turning to God when you are poor in spirit knowing that you will be met with grace, comfort, and love?

   ....
   ....
   ....

5. Why is it comforting to know that God never breaks or forgets the covenant He made with His people? How does this impact how you view each day?

   ....
   ....
   ....

JOURNAL
your thoughts

JOURNAL
your thoughts

WEEK 4

"*Glory* to God in the highest, and on earth *peace* among *people* with whom he is pleased!"

Luke 2:14

PRAY

Write down your prayer requests and praises for this week.

....
....
....
....
....
....
....
....
....
....
....
....
....
....

WEEKLY CHALLENGE

As we finish our study this week with the angels' song, ask yourself what you can do to grow in your knowledge of God's glory. Most of all, pray that God will increasingly open the eyes of your heart to His glorious holiness. You may find it helpful to pray Paul's prayer in Ephesians 3:16-21 for yourself. Also, continue memorizing Mary's song. Review what you memorized the last three weeks and begin memorizing the last portion, Luke 1:54-55.

....
....
....
....
....
....

WEEK 4
Monday

READ

Luke 2:1-20

Now in those days a decree went out from Caesar Augustus to register all the empire for taxes. 2 This was the first registration, taken when Quirinius was governor of Syria. 3 Everyone went to his own town to be registered. 4 So Joseph also went up from the town of Nazareth in Galilee to Judea, to the city of David called Bethlehem, because he was of the house and family line of David. 5 He went to be registered with Mary, who was promised in marriage to him, and who was expecting a child. 6 While they were there, the time came for her to deliver her child. 7 And she gave birth to her firstborn son and wrapped him in strips of cloth and laid him in a manger, because there was no place for them in the inn. 8 Now there were shepherds nearby living out in the field, keeping guard over their flock at night. 9 An angel of the Lord appeared to them, and the glory of the Lord shone around them, and they were absolutely terrified. 10 But the angel said to them, "Do not be afraid! Listen carefully, for I proclaim to you good news that brings great joy to all the people: 11 Today your Savior is born in the city of David. He is Christ the Lord. 12 This will be a sign for you: You will find a baby wrapped in strips of cloth and lying in a manger." 13 Suddenly a vast, heavenly army appeared with the angel, praising God and saying, 14 "Glory to God in the highest, and on earth peace among people with whom he is pleased!" 15 When the angels left them and went back to heaven, the shepherds said to one another, "Let us go over to Bethlehem and see this thing that has taken place, that the Lord has made

WEEK 4
Monday

Luke 2:1-20 (continued)

known to us." 16 So they hurried off and located Mary and Joseph, and found the baby lying in a manger. 17 When they saw him, they related what they had been told about this child, 18 and all who heard it were astonished at what the shepherds said. 19 But Mary treasured up all these words, pondering in her heart what they might mean. 20 So the shepherds returned, glorifying and praising God for all they had heard and seen; everything was just as they had been told.

2 Corinthians 8:9

For you know the grace of our Lord Jesus Christ, that although he was rich, he became poor for your sakes, so that you by his poverty could become rich.

Philippians 2:5-11

You should have the same attitude toward one another that Christ Jesus had, 6 who, though he existed in the form of God, did not regard equality with God as something to be grasped, 7 but emptied himself by taking on the form of a slave, by looking like other men, and by sharing in human nature. 8 He humbled himself by becoming obedient to the point of death —even death on a cross! 9 As a result God highly exalted him and gave him the name that is above every name, 10 so that at the name of Jesus every knee will bow —in heaven and on earth and under the earth— 11 and every tongue confess that Jesus Christ is Lord to the glory of God the Father.

Even if we are overlooked or even rejected, we can trust that God sees us.

SOAP

WEEK 4 · MONDAY

SOAP / *2 Corinthians 8:9*
SCRIPTURE / *Write out the SOAP verses*

OBSERVATION / *Write 3 - 4 observations*

APPLICATION / *Write down 1 - 2 applications*

PRAYER / *Write out a prayer over what you learned*

DEVOTION
WEEK 4 • MONDAY

SOAP

2 Corinthians 8:9

"For you know the grace of our Lord Jesus Christ, that although he was rich, he became poor for your sakes, so that you by his poverty could become rich."

INTO THE TEXT

It is truly amazing to think of the conditions Jesus was born in. Poor Joseph couldn't find a better place to stay for the night, so Mary had to give birth in a dirty stable. Imagine a young woman going through labor in the midst of the smell of animals and hay having nothing but a cow's feeding troth to place her baby in. There was not the slightest sign of glory or majesty when God's Son entered this world.

The second part of the nativity story talks about the shepherds in the field. This is where we would expect poverty, roughness, and the smell of animals - certainly nothing awesome. And yet, it is here that we find glory, a bright light from heaven and a great choir of angels singing. We learn something very important in this "reversal of events." Through the birth of Jesus, our human poverty fell on Him while His eternal glory came to us.

Before being born on this earth, Jesus was in God's eternal world, where there was no pain, sickness, fear, or crying. It was a world where there was only light, peace, and joy. But then He entered our world where He would experience hunger, tiredness, rejection, and unbelievable suffering. He took on a human body, which could be beaten and spat on. He experienced a body with sensitive nerve endings and pain, especially the excruciating pain of being whipped and nail-pierced, as well as a body which could enter into the darkness of death.

Why was He willing to do it? It is proclaimed by the angel. Jesus wanted to enter into our fear and hardship, so we don't have to be afraid anymore. He came into our sadness in order to give us His joy. He became a humble servant in order to make us children of the King. He became poor in order to make us rich. He gave up heaven in order to give us heaven. What a wonderful Savior!

PRAYER

Lord Jesus, you left heaven in order to give me yourself. Help me understand your love for me in a deeper way. Amen.

WEEK 4
Tuesday

READ

Luke 2:13-14

Suddenly a vast, heavenly army appeared with the angel, praising God and saying, 14 "Glory to God in the highest, and on earth peace among people with whom he is pleased!"

1 Peter 1:10-12

Concerning this salvation, the prophets who predicted the grace that would come to you searched and investigated carefully. 11 They probed into what person or time the Spirit of Christ within them was indicating when he testified beforehand about the sufferings appointed for Christ and his subsequent glory. 12 They were shown that they were serving not themselves but you, in regard to the things now announced to you through those who proclaimed the gospel to you by the Holy Spirit sent from heaven—things angels long to catch a glimpse of.

Revelation 5:6-14

Then I saw standing in the middle of the throne and of the four living creatures, and in the middle of the elders, a Lamb that appeared to have been killed. He had seven horns and seven eyes, which are the seven spirits of God sent out into all the earth. 7 Then he came and took the scroll from the right hand of the one who was seated on the throne, 8 and when he had taken the scroll, the four living creatures and the twenty-four elders threw themselves to the ground before the Lamb. Each of them had a harp and golden bowls full of incense (which are the prayers of the saints). 9 They were singing a new song: "You are worthy to take the scroll and to open its seals because you were killed, and at the cost of your own blood you have purchased for God persons from every tribe, language, people, and nation. 10 You have appointed them as a kingdom and priests to serve our God, and they will reign on the earth." 11 Then I looked and heard the voice of many angels in a circle around the throne, as well as the living creatures and the elders. Their number was ten thousand times ten thousand—thousands times thousands— 12 all of whom were singing in a loud voice: "Worthy is the lamb who was killed to receive power and wealth and wisdom and might and honor and glory and praise!" 13 Then I heard every creature—in heaven, on earth, under the earth, in the sea, and all that is in them—singing: "To the one seated on the throne and to the Lamb be praise, honor, glory, and ruling power forever and ever!" 14 And the four living creatures were saying "Amen," and the elders threw themselves to the ground and worshiped.

SOAP
WEEK 4 · TUESDAY

SOAP / *Luke 2:13*
SCRIPTURE / *Write out the SOAP verses*

OBSERVATION / *Write 3 - 4 observations*

APPLICATION / *Write down 1 - 2 applications*

PRAYER / *Write out a prayer over what you learned*

DEVOTION
WEEK 4 • TUESDAY

SOAP

Luke 2:13

"Suddenly a vast, heavenly army appeared with the angel, praising God and saying,"

INTO THE TEXT

What the shepherds saw must have been truly awesome. This was not the Roman army they knew and dreaded with its shimmering armor, shields, spears, and swords. This was God's vast heavenly army, an army larger, brighter, and more glorious than anything they had ever seen.

Yet, this was an army not sent to fight against God's rebellious subjects but to announce the news of a Savior. The angels not only proclaimed Jesus' birth but they were so filled with joy that they burst into song, praising God together. Have you ever wondered why the angels were singing? After all, it wasn't for them that Jesus was born. What filled them with such praise?

Since their creation, angels, as God's messengers, have seen God's face and been deeply interested in everything He does. They love what God loves and hate what He hates. They know very well that man's sin brought terrible suffering on the whole creation. They saw Adam and Eve disobey their Creator and lose fellowship with Him. And they heard God's merciful promise to send a Redeemer, but they did not know how He was going to do it. God had not revealed His plan, even to the angels.

It must have been so astonishing to them when they saw the plan, this old mystery, unfold before their eyes. The second person of the Trinity, God the Son, becomes a human being. How was it possible for two natures so infinitely different, the divine and human, to be united in one person? How could the eternal God become a servant under the law and obey it perfectly on behalf of humans? How could a divine person suffer pain and death? How could Jesus, who is infinitely loved by the Father, come under His judgment?

The angels praised God for this amazing plan of salvation. They knew what a privilege it was for God to give to humans by opening the door into heaven for them. They were rejoicing that Jesus would rescue many people from an eternity in hell. As Jesus says in Luke 15, angels rejoice over even one person who repents and turns to God. If angels rejoice over this, how much more should we, for whom the Savior was sent.

PRAYER

Heavenly Father, help me to daily rejoice over your plan of salvation in my life and the life of others as the angels did at the birth of Jesus. Amen.

WEEK 4
Wednesday

READ

Luke 2:9-14

An angel of the Lord appeared to them, and the glory of the Lord shone around them, and they were absolutely terrified. 10 But the angel said to them, "Do not be afraid! Listen carefully, for I proclaim to you good news that brings great joy to all the people: 11 Today your Savior is born in the city of David. He is Christ the Lord. 12 This will be a sign for you: You will find a baby wrapped in strips of cloth and lying in a manger." 13 Suddenly a vast, heavenly army appeared with the angel, praising God and saying, 14 "Glory to God in the highest, and on earth peace among people with whom he is pleased!"

Hebrews 1:1-3

After God spoke long ago in various portions and in various ways to our ancestors through the prophets, 2 in these last days he has spoken to us in a son, whom he appointed heir of all things, and through whom he created the world. 3 The Son is the radiance of his glory and the representation of his essence, and he sustains all things by his powerful word, and so when he had accomplished cleansing for sins, *he sat down at the right hand of the Majesty on high.*

John 1:14

Now the Word became flesh and took up residence among us. We saw his glory—the glory of the one and only, full of grace and truth, who came from the Father.

SOAP

WEEK 4 · WEDNESDAY

SOAP / *John 1:14*
SCRIPTURE / *Write out the SOAP verses*

OBSERVATION / *Write 3 - 4 observations*

APPLICATION / *Write down 1 - 2 applications*

PRAYER / *Write out a prayer over what you learned*

DEVOTION
WEEK 4 • WEDNESDAY

SOAP

John 1:14

"Now the Word became flesh and took up residence among us. We saw his glory—the glory of the one and only, full of grace and truth, who came from the Father."

INTO THE TEXT

God's glory is often mentioned in the Bible and refers to the visible demonstration of His own excellence, His holiness. Through the birth of Jesus, the angels could see the glory of God clearly. They realized that this plan of salvation demonstrated God's glory more than anything He had ever done before.

Each one of God's attributes is perfectly portrayed and glorified in the life of Jesus. We can see God's power on full display because He perfectly united Jesus' divine and human nature in one person. He also shows us that He - and He alone - is able to save people and change their sinful nature. We can see God's justice, that He would not let any sin (no matter how small) go unpunished. He demonstrated to us how much He hates sin when He put His beloved Son through a horrible death. And we can see His words never fail. Everything Jesus did was in fulfillment of God's promises.

But most of all, by sending Jesus, God demonstrated His love and mercy. God showed to the angels and the whole human race that He has a heart of love even towards those who sin against Him. By doing so, He has given us the greatest gift possible. He has given us Himself. The angels rejoiced to serve such a loving and merciful God.

God delights to show us His glory. Just like the angels, the extent to which we see His glory will be the measure by which we are filled with joy ourselves. It's what God made us for, to glorify Him and to enjoy Him forever. When God glorifies Himself, it is for our greatest joy and benefit. The angels' happiness - as well as our own - comes from seeing the glory of God.

PRAYER

Lord, let me see your glory more and more. May my whole life glorify your name. Amen.

WEEK 4
Thursday

READ

Luke 2:14

"Glory to God in the highest, and on earth peace among people with whom he is pleased!"

Romans 5:1-11

Therefore, since we have been declared righteous by faith, we have peace with God through our Lord Jesus Christ, 2 through whom we have also obtained access into this grace in which we stand, and we rejoice in the hope of God's glory. 3 Not only this, but we also rejoice in sufferings, knowing that suffering produces endurance, 4 and endurance, character, and character, hope. 5 And hope does not disappoint, because the love of God has been poured out in our hearts through the Holy Spirit who was given to us. 6 For while we were still helpless, at the right time Christ died for the ungodly. 7 (For rarely will anyone die for a righteous person, though for a good person perhaps someone might possibly dare to die.) 8 But God demonstrates his own love for us, in that while we were still sinners, Christ died for us. 9 Much more then, because we have now been declared righteous by his blood, we will be saved through him from God's wrath. 10 For if while we were enemies we were reconciled to God through the death of his Son, how much more, since we have been reconciled, will we be saved by his life? 11 Not only this, but we also rejoice in God through our Lord Jesus Christ, through whom we have now received this reconciliation.

Isaiah 9:6

For a child has been born to us, a son has been given to us. He shoulders responsibility and is called Wonderful Adviser, Mighty God, Everlasting Father, Prince of Peace.

SOAP

WEEK 4 • THURSDAY

SOAP / *Luke 2:14*
SCRIPTURE / *Write out the SOAP verses*

OBSERVATION / *Write 3 - 4 observations*

APPLICATION / *Write down 1 - 2 applications*

PRAYER / *Write out a prayer over what you learned*

DEVOTION
WEEK 4 · THURSDAY

SOAP

Luke 2:14

"Glory to God in the highest, and on earth peace among people with whom he is pleased!"

INTO THE TEXT

The angels' joyful proclamation of "peace on earth" is great news for us. The Prince of Peace, Jesus Christ, has finally come to bring God's peace to our lost world.

Who is this peace for? According to the angels, it is only for those with whom God is pleased. Even though God's offer of peace goes out to everyone, most ignore it, choosing instead to continue in their rebellion. Some may not even be aware that they are God's enemies. But by turning away from His Word and living life the way they want, they reject Him. There is no peace apart from God.

On the other hand, there are those who have been drawn to Jesus, who have accepted God's offer of peace through His Son by admitting their sin, turning from it, and receiving His forgiveness. With such people, God is pleased. To them, He gives His peace.

There are days I feel very restless and wonder how a holy God could possibly be pleased with someone like me. I can be very negative, fail often, talk too much, lose my temper, and certainly feel no peace or joyful tranquility in my heart. This is when I need to remember that the only reason God is pleased with me is because of His Son, Jesus. When God looks at me, He looks at the perfect life of Jesus. I am sinful, yet I am God's beloved daughter. I don't do enough, yet He is satisfied with me. I am "in Christ," hidden in His righteousness. How did I get there? By faith.

If I want to experience true peace, I need faith. As Paul says in Romans 15:13, God will fill us with peace as we believe in Him. I need faith that regards all my own works as worthless and sinful but Jesus' work for me as more than enough. I need a faith that tells God every fear and anxiety, knowing that He will take care of me because He is for me. It's only when I believe His promises and become confident of His love towards me that my restless soul finds true peace.

PRAYER

Jesus, you see my restless heart. Give me faith to trust in you and fill me with your peace. Amen.

WEEK 4
Friday

READ

Luke 2:15-20

When the angels left them and went back to heaven, the shepherds said to one another, "Let us go over to Bethlehem and see this thing that has taken place, that the Lord has made known to us." 16 So they hurried off and located Mary and Joseph, and found the baby lying in a manger. 17 When they saw him, they related what they had been told about this child, 18 and all who heard it were astonished at what the shepherds said. 19 But Mary treasured up all these words, pondering in her heart what they might mean. 20 So the shepherds returned, glorifying and praising God for all they had heard and seen; everything was just as they had been told.

Philippians 2:9-11

As a result God highly exalted him and gave him the name that is above every name, 10 so that at the name of Jesus every knee will bow —in heaven and on earth and under the earth— 11 and every tongue confess that Jesus Christ is Lord to the glory of God the Father.

Revelation 15:1-4

Then I saw another great and astounding sign in heaven: seven angels who have seven final plagues (they are final because in them God's anger is completed). 2 Then I saw something like a sea of glass mixed with fire, and those who had conquered the beast and his image and the number of his name. They were standing by the sea of glass, holding harps given to them by God. 3 They sang the song of Moses the servant of God and the song of the Lamb: "Great and astounding are your deeds, Lord God, the All-Powerful! Just and true are your ways, King over the nations! 4 Who will not fear you, O Lord, and glorify your name, because you alone are holy? All nations will come and worship before you for your righteous acts have been revealed."

SOAP
WEEK 4 · FRIDAY

SOAP / *Philippians 2:9-11*
SCRIPTURE / *Write out the SOAP verses*

OBSERVATION / *Write 3 - 4 observations*

APPLICATION / *Write down 1 - 2 applications*

PRAYER / *Write out a prayer over what you learned*

DEVOTION
WEEK 4 · FRIDAY

SOAP

Philippians 2:9-11

"As a result God highly exalted him and gave him the name that is above every name, so that at the name of Jesus every knee will bow —in heaven and on earth and under the earth— and every tongue confess that Jesus Christ is Lord to the glory of God the Father."

INTO THE TEXT

The glory which the shepherds had seen in the fields did not last very long. When the angels went back to heaven, it was dark again. The night was quiet, and the sheep continued grazing. But these men's lives were not the same. After they had gone to see Jesus, we are told that they "returned, glorifying and praising God for all the things they had heard and seen." God's glory had come into their hearts, just as it comes into the heart of every Christian.

We have spent four weeks rejoicing along with the Advent songs of the gospel of Luke. We have learned from Zechariah, Simeon, Mary, and the angels. Together with them, we have seen some of God's glory when we look at His wonderful attributes, His holiness, strength, tender mercy, and compassion. May we remember this glory and grow more and more in the knowledge of Him. May we do so with singing in our hearts.

May we experience true joy in our Savior, who came on that first Christmas over 2000 years ago. We know that He has done the most important work at His first coming, carrying our sins away and defeating our enemy.

May we trust Him who continues to come to us daily in all our worries and pain. He is our best friend, our Prince of Peace, and our comforter. We can pour out our hearts to Him and look to Him for help.

May we patiently wait for Him who will soon come back in power and majesty. The next time He comes, He will judge all those who have rejected His mercy, who were too proud and self-sufficient to turn to Him. And He will take His own, those who have fled to him for shelter, to enjoy His glory in heaven forever.

Until then, let's live like the shepherds and tell many other people about Jesus, the wonderful Savior who loved us so much that He left heaven to come to us.

PRAYER

Lord Jesus, thank you for coming to us that first Christmas. Let your glory shine brightly in my heart today and in this coming year. As I wait for your glorious return, let me be a witness and tell others about you. Amen.

REFLECT

WEEK 4

1. What are some of the things Jesus came to give us in order to make us children of God?

   ....
   ....
   ....

2. How can you begin to cultivate a life of praise and rejoicing over who Jesus is and what He did for you?

   ....
   ....
   ....

3. Are you looking forward to seeing God's glory in heaven? Why? Where have you seen God's glory on display in your life lately?

   ....
   ....
   ....

4. What do you need in order to experience the true peace found in Christ? How can you begin practicing this today?

   ....
   ....
   ....

5. Why do you think it is important to grow in the knowledge of the glory of Jesus, especially as we seek to tell others about Him? Who is someone in your sphere of influence that you can share the good news of the gospel with this week?

   ....
   ....
   ....

JOURNAL
your thoughts

JOURNAL
your thoughts

Join Us

ONLINE
lovegodgreatly.com

SHOP
lovegodgreatly.com

FACEBOOK
Love God Greatly

INSTAGRAM
@lovegodgreatlyofficial

APP
Love God Greatly

....

CONTACT US
info@lovegodgreatly.com

CONNECT
#LoveGodGreatly

FOR YOU

WHAT WE OFFER

45+ Translations	Love God Greatly Journal
Bible Reading Plans	Bible Study Journals
Online Bible Study	Community Groups
Love God Greatly App	Love God Greatly Bible
Over 200 Countries Served	Young Women Love God Greatly Bible

TOPICAL BIBLE STUDIES

The Importance of Prayer	The God Who Restores
Trusting God in the Midst of Suffering	Not Made to be Alone
Beautifully Surrendered	Enduring Hope
Come, Lord Jesus, Come	Armor of God
Fear and Anxiety	The Promised Messiah

STUDIES ON BOOKS OF THE BIBLE

Choosing God Instead of the World
A Study on Genesis

Our Security for Eternity
A Study on the Gospel of John

He Sees, He Knows, He Cares
A Study on the Gospel of Luke

From Broken to Restored
A Study on Nehemiah

To find even more topical studies and studies on books of the Bible, visit us online. Also check out our corresponding kids resources!

LOVEGODGREATLY.COM

YOUNG WOMEN'S
LOVE GOD GREATLY BIBLE

The NET Young Women's LGG Bible is a transformative resource tailored for young women. Uncover the richness of Scripture with detailed maps and timelines. Immerse yourself in 50 SOAP reading plans, 100 inspiring devotions, 66 personal testimonies, and more! This beautifully crafted Bible helps build your faith, providing a beautiful guide for the spiritual journey of young women.

STORE.LOVEGODGREATLY.COM

Scan to Shop

Printed in Great Britain
by Amazon